Devotions for Hurting Hearts

A Study of the Gospel of John Chapters 13–16
For those who have lost loved ones

The Lord is near to the brokenhearted,
And saves those who are crushed in spirit.
Psalm 34:18

By Robert James Walker

WESTBOW
PRESS®
A DIVISION OF THOMAS NELSON
& ZONDERVAN

WestBow Press books may be ordered through booksellers or by contacting:

WestBow Press
A Division of Thomas Nelson & Zondervan
1663 Liberty Drive
Bloomington, IN 47403
www.westbowpress.com
1 (866) 928-1240

Scripture quotations are taken from The New American Standard Bible®, Copyright © 1960, 1962, 1963, 1968, 1971, 1972, 1973, 1975, 1977, 1995 by The Lockman Foundation. Used by permission.

ISBN: 978-1-9736-5384-4 (sc)
ISBN: 978-1-9736-5385-1 (e)

Print information available on the last page.

WestBow Press rev. date: 6/25/2019

Introduction

Isaiah 53:3; He was despised and forsaken of men, a man of sorrows, and acquainted with grief.

What a blessed Comforter we have in Jesus. Because He is "a man of sorrows and acquainted with grief" He is more than able to sympathize with and minister to our hurting hearts. On the occasion of the Last Supper the Apostle John in chapters 13-16 of his Gospel shares some of the words and deeds of Jesus on the eve of His death on a cross. Jesus spends this tender and intimate evening to share His love, and prepare His disciples for the grief and sorrow that they would experience over the course of the next three days. He also teaches them how to carry on after His departure. When I studied these Scriptures I encountered Jesus in a new and refreshing way that blessed my heart. These Scriptures helped me deal with some of the issues that I was struggling with as a result of my wife Linda's departure to Heaven six months prior to the writing of these devotions. These devotions were written to minister comfort to and strengthen the faith of other grievers. They are designed to help you focus on who Jesus is and the blessed life that Jesus has planned for you. These devotions are intended to be read on a day to day basis. Set time aside each day to read one and spend time with Jesus in prayer.

My prayer for you dear reader is from Paul's Epistle to the Ephesians 3:14-21; *For this reason, I bow my knees before the Father, from whom every family in heaven and on earth derives its name, that He would grant you, according to the riches of his glory, to be strengthened with power through His Spirit in the inner man; so that Christ may dwell in your hearts through faith; and that you, being rooted and grounded in love, may be able to comprehend with all the saints what is the breadth and length and height and depth, and to know the love of Christ which surpasses knowledge, that you may be filled up to all the fulness of God. Now to Him who is able to do exceeding abundantly beyond all that we ask or think, according to the power that works within us, to Him be the glory in the church and in Christ Jesus to all generations, forever and ever. Amen.* The weight of the burden of grief is often too heavy for us to bear alone. Fortunately, we are never alone. Jesus and everything He provides us is constantly available to help lift us up and pull us through.

Since then that we have a great high priest who has passed through the heavens, Jesus the Son of God, let us hold fast our confession. For we do not have a high priest who cannot sympathize with our weaknesses; but One who has been tempted in all things as we are, yet without sin. Let us therefore draw near with confidence to the throne of grace, that we may receive mercy and may find grace to help in time of need, Hebrews 4:14-16. Go often to the throne of grace. Do not let anything keep you away. May God richly bless you as you continue to read and seek the Father of mercies and the God of all comfort.

John 13:1: *Now before the Feast of the Passover, Jesus knowing that His hour had come that He should depart out of this world to the Father, having loved His own who were in the world, He loved them to the end.*

There are two points that I would like to observe from this verse. The first is, Jesus knew where He was going, "to the Father". Jesus also knew that His disciples, "His own", would be left behind in this world. They would witness His arrest, His crucifixion, His resurrection, and His ascension into Heaven. In love Jesus prepares "His own" for what they were about to go through. This includes the terrible grief they would experience as a result of His departure and their loss. The focus of this verse, however, is not on what was about to happen to Jesus on this earth, but the focus is on His final destination, "to the Father". You see death was not the end for Jesus and neither will it be for those who put their faith in Him. On Friday morning, July 24th, 2009, my wife Linda departed from this world and woke up in the presence of our heavenly Father. Unlike Jesus she did not know that she was going to leave, but like Jesus she also knew her final destination, "to the Father". I am comforted by the knowledge that she is rejoicing in the arms of the Father.

The second point is, Jesus "loved His own". John 1:12-13 proclaims, *But as many as received Him (Jesus), to them gave He gave the right to become children of God, even to those who believe in His name, who were born not of blood, nor of the will of the flesh, nor of the will of man, but of God.* If you have received Jesus you are "born of God" and are therefore "His own". You can be comforted by the blessed truth that Jesus loves you. *But God demonstrates His own love toward us, in that while we were yet sinners, Christ died for us, Romans 5:8.* I have but one child, a daughter who I love dearly and would never sacrifice for anyone in this world. But that is exactly what God did for us helpless sinners. *But God, being rich in mercy, because of His great love with which He loved us, even when we were dead in our transgressions, made us alive together with Christ (by grace you have been saved) Ephesians 2:4-5.* No one loves us like God does. Romans 8:35, 38-39 promises, *Who shall separate us from the love of Christ? Shall tribulation, or distress, or persecution, or famine, or nakedness, or peril, or sword? For I am convinced that neither death, nor life, nor angels, nor principalities, nor things present, nor things to come, nor powers, nor height, nor depth, nor any other created thing, shall be able to separate us from the love of God, which is in Christ Jesus our Lord.* Although you may feel like God has abandoned you or that He has hurt you by taking your loved one away, Jesus is still there right where you need Him and He still cares about you. Nothing that we can ever go through, including the loss of a loved one, can ever separate us from God's love.

Prayer: Father thank you for the comfort in knowing that our loved one who knew you is now rejoicing in your presence. And thank you for your unfailing love that will not let us go and blesses us in our darkest moments. In Jesus' precious name; Amen.

The Refreshing Ministry of Jesus, John 13:3-5

John 13:3-5: *Jesus, knowing that the Father had given all things into His hands, and that He had come forth from God, and was going back to God, rose from supper, and laid aside His garments; and taking a towel, He girded Himself about. Then He poured water into a basin, and began to wash the disciples' feet, and to wipe them with the towel with which He was girded.*

I believe that to fully grasp what is happening here it is important to ask this question. Who is Jesus? To answer we will start at the first chapter of John verses 1-3, where we learn that Jesus was "the Word" who existed in the beginning with God and who as God created all things. In verse 14 Jesus "became flesh and dwelt among us". In verse 29 John the Baptist points to Jesus as "the Lamb of God who takes away the sin of the World"!, and in verse 33 he proclaims Jesus as "the one who baptizes with the Holy Spirit". In John chapter 5: 25-26 we learn that Jesus has the power to raise the dead and the authority to execute judgment. To sum up Jesus is God the Creator, who became man, who became the sacrifice for our sins, who baptizes us with his Holy Spirit, and who will raise and judge the dead.

"Therefore also God highly exalted Him, and bestowed on Him a name which is above every name, that at the name of Jesus every knee should bow, of those who are in heaven, and on earth, and under the earth, and that every tongue should confess that Jesus Christ is Lord, to the glory of God the Father." Philippians 2:9-11.

It is this Jesus, the Lord of all creation, who humbly takes the place of a servant to bow at His disciples' feet to wash all twenty-four of them, including the two who will in the next moment run to betray Him. Jesus takes the time to minister His love in a very physical way that would be cleansing, soothing and comforting. One of my fondest memories of camping with youth was a time when our leader decided to hold a voluntary foot washing. One of the youth chose to wash my feet. My feet were dirty, smelly, battered, and sore from three days of trekking around the mountains in the summer heat. It was not a pleasant task for the youth, but to me it was so soothing, so comforting, and so therapeutic that I have never forgotten the experience. In a similar way our souls are dirty, bruised and battered by the loss of our loved one. Our hearts may be troubled by bad thoughts, negative emotions, sinful desires and harmful behaviors that make our grieving experience unbearable. Jesus wants to come and minister His love to us, to cleanse and heal us like no one else can. *"But when the kindness of God our Savior and His love for mankind appeared, He saved us, not on the basis of deeds which we have done in righteousness, but according to His mercy, by the washing of regeneration and renewing by the Holy Spirit, who He poured out upon us richly through Jesus Christ our Savior." Titus 3:4-6*

Jesus wants to "wash your feet". The gospel records that when Jesus came to the disciple Peter, he protested, but Jesus persisted and Peter submitted and received the blessing. All we need to do is to submit to the love of Jesus and let Him have His way with us.

Prayer: Dear Jesus. Please come to my wounded and hurting heart and minister your love to me as you did to your disciples. Pour out the regenerating and restoring baptism of your Holy Spirit. Have your perfect way with me as I trust in you. Amen.

John 13:14-15, *"If I then, the Lord and the Teacher, washed your feet, you also ought to wash one another's feet. For I gave you an example that you also should do as I did to you."*

As grieving souls we have a tendency to focus on our own sorrow and our own loss. This is understandable when we are travelling through "the valley of the shadow of death" but this is not the example of Jesus. While He was facing His own cup of suffering He reaches out and meets the needs of others. *"Do nothing from selfishness or empty conceit, but with humility of mind let each of you regard one another as more important than himself; do not merely look out for your own personal interests, but also for the interests of others." Philippians 2:3-4.* This high calling to a lowly position may seem impossible when your world is collapsing around you, but if you reach beyond your pain to help another hurting soul it does wonders to help heal your hurting heart. A disabled friend of mine was going through a deep trial just a few months after my wife passed. She had an entire storage bin full of her belongings that needed to be moved to her new house. Because of some sinful things that were going on in her family people were reluctant to get involved, so I was the only one available to do the job. It was a long hard day and I was exhausted at the end of it. Not many people knew about it. I did not receive anything for my labor except a heartfelt thank you from my friend, but the experience helped me climb out of the miry pit of self pity that I had sunk into.

Recently I joined a grief support group that meets weekly. At first it was a blessing to share my burden of grief with the other members of the group and receive their support, encouragement, and comfort. But as I continued to attend and new members joined the group I had the blessed opportunity to reach out and comfort those hurting souls with the comfort that I had received. *"Blessed be the God and Father of our Lord Jesus Christ, the Father of mercies and the God of all comfort; who comforts us in all our affliction so that we may be able to comfort those who are in any affliction with the comfort with which we ourselves are comforted of God." 2 Corinthians 1:3-4.* As a member of the body of Christ we are to, *"Rejoice with those who rejoice, and weep with those who weep. Be of the same mind toward one another; do not be haughty of mind, but associate with the lowly. Do not be wise in your own estimation." Romans 12:15-16.* Death is a frequent occurrence in our fallen world. As a result there are many other souls who are suffering from the loss of a loved one and need the comfort and support of others to help them carry on. A grief support group can be a wonderful place for them to come and get their "feet washed". *"Bear one another's burdens, and thus fulfill the law of Christ." Galatians 6:2.*

Prayer: Dear Lord and Teacher; Thank you for the example of your humble servitude. Strengthen our hearts so that we may be able to support and comfort others with the comfort that you have comforted us. Give us wisdom to know what to say and do and the gentleness of your Holy Spirit for every situation. May You be glorified and others drawn to You as we live out Your example until You come. Amen.

John 13:31-32: *When therefore he (Judas) had gone out, Jesus said, "Now is the Son of Man glorified, and God is glorified in Him; if God is glorified in Him, God will also glorify Him in Himself, and will glorify Him immediately."*

The glory of Jesus Messiah was to be crucified on a cruel Roman cross. Speaking of this glory Jesus says in John 12:24; *"Truly, truly, I say to you, unless a grain of wheat falls into the earth and dies, it remains by itself alone; but if it dies, it bears much fruit."* It was Jesus' intent to bear much fruit by shedding His blood on the cross. In John 3:14-15 Jesus promises, *"And as Moses lifted up the serpent in the wilderness, even so must the Son of Man be lifted up; that whosoever believes may in Him have eternal life."* The purpose of the bronze serpent of Moses was to save the children of Israel who were bitten by deadly poisonous serpents. They needed only to look upon the bronze serpent to live. In the same way Jesus was lifted up upon a cross so that all who believe in Him should be saved from the poison of their sin and receive His eternal life. Since then, many hell bound sinners have looked to the Savior who died on a cross to save them and give them eternal life. The promise still stands, *"for, 'Whoever will call upon the name of the Lord will be saved.'" Romans 10:13.* The cross of Jesus stands as the most glorious act of love and mercy ever committed in the history of mankind.

On the occasion of my wife Linda's memorial service, many of her friends stood up and shared about the wonderful things she had done and what a blessing she had been to them. Linda was honored as a woman who loved the Lord by giving of herself to others. But the honor and glory bestowed upon her that evening pales in comparison to the rewards that will be showered upon her by the King of Kings and Lord of Lords. Based on the testimony I know of how she lived her life I am sure Linda will hear words like these from her Lord Jesus; *"Well done, good and faithful slave; you were faithful with a few things, I will put you in charge of many things, enter into the joy of your lord." Matthew 25:21.*

You see dear ones, death is not where we are finally defeated. Death will be our most glorious victory in Jesus. Your loved one who died in Jesus has greater things in store for them than anything they ever received in this world. A greater glory awaits the faithful followers of Jesus. *"Therefore, since we have so great a cloud of witnesses surrounding us, let us also lay aside every encumbrance, and the sin which so easily entangles us, and let us run with endurance the race that is set before us, fixing our eyes on Jesus, the author and perfecter of faith, who for the joy set before Him endured the cross, despising the shame, and has sat down at the right hand of the throne of God." Hebrews 12:1-2.*

Prayer: Dear Heavenly Father; Thank you again for the love and mercy of your Son Jesus, who sacrificed Himself on a cross to redeem us and make us your own. And thank you for all the faithful ones, who endured the race and showed us the way to you. Thank you that they are there with you at the throne of God ever witnessing to those of us still enduring the race. Help us keep our eyes on the Author and Perfecter of our faith until we reach the glorious finish line where Jesus Himself eagerly waits to reward us. In His Glorious name we pray, Amen

John 13:33; *Little children, I am with you a little while longer. You shall seek Me; and as I said to the Jews, I now say to you also, "Where I am going, you cannot come."*

In 43 days from the time Jesus spoke these words He would be physically separated from His disciples. They would watch Him go away into the clouds. The Bible records the event in Acts 1:9-11. *And after He had said these things, He was lifted up while they were looking on, and a cloud received Him out of their sight. And as they were gazing intently into the sky while He was departing, behold two men in white clothing stood beside them; and they also said, "Men of Galilee, why do you stand looking into the sky? This Jesus, who has been taken up from you into heaven, will come in just the same way as you have watched Him go into heaven."* The disciples had followed Jesus for about three years from the Sea of Galilee to Jerusalem and everywhere in between. Like sheep following their shepherd, Jesus took them wherever He went. Now their Shepherd ascends into the clouds and they are left "gazing intently into the sky" probably wondering what was going to happen next. Jesus is gone and questions must have abounded in their heads. Where will we go? Who will lead us? Who will take care of us and teach us? How are we going to live now? It must have been terribly traumatic for the disciples to be suddenly separated from Jesus. They could not fly. Gravity kept their feet planted on the ground. And without Jesus they faced a huge void in their lives.

When my wife, Linda, was here with me we were inseparable. Like perfectively matched oxen we were yoked together to shoulder all of life's burdens. Now she is *absent from the body and at home with the Lord"* where I cannot go. This separation has left a big hole in my life. There is an empty seat next to me in church every Sunday and another one in our van when I travel. There is no one to enthusiastically greet me every day when I get home with hugs and kisses. And no one who asks how was it today and genuinely wants to know. I miss her head resting on my chest at night and her bright smile that said she was excited about having me around. No more love, no more laughter, no more silly playfulness, and no more quiet walks hand in hand on the beach. She is gone and I am left here gazing intently into the sky crying out, "Where are you?" The answer is an awful dead silence.

Fortunately this separation although intense is not eternal. The blessed words of the angels from Acts 1:11 offer comfort and great hope; *"This Jesus, who has been taken up from you into heaven, will come in just the same way as you have watched Him go into heaven."* Oh blessed thought, Jesus is coming again and shall bring our loved ones who abide in heaven with Him. "When we all get to heaven, what a day of rejoicing that will be! When we all see Jesus, we'll sing and shout the victory!" We have a most wonderful reunion to look forward to! Halleluiah! Praise God!

Prayer: Heavenly Father: What a terrible time it must have been for the disciples when Jesus left this earth. But what a blessing it must have been for you to have Him home. Likewise our loss is also unbearable, but your gain is great. Lord, *"Put my tears in Thy bottle; Are they not in your book?" Psalm 56:8.* Thank you for sending your angels to encourage your disciples, and thank you that their words give hope for us today. Even so Lord Jesus, come quickly! " Amen.

The Greatest Command of Jesus — Love One Another, John 13:34-35

John 13:34-35: *"A new commandment I give to you, that you love one another, even as I have loved you, that you also love another. By this all men will know that you are My disciples, if you have love for one another."*

Jesus sets the highest standard for His disciple's love when he commands, "love one another, even as I have loved you." In order to understand how we are to obey Jesus' command, we first must ask, what was His example of love? In Ephesians 5:25-27 we read; *Husbands, love your wives, just as Christ also loved the church and gave himself up for her; that He might sanctify her, having cleansed her by the washing of water with the word, that He might present to Himself the church in all her glory, having no spot or wrinkle or any such thing; but that she should be holy and blameless.* Jesus chose the twelve disciples like a bridegroom chooses his bride. He called them to leave their homes, their families, and their businesses to follow Him for the rest of their lives. Jesus lived sacrificially to provide for their every need, He protected them, taught them, corrected them, empowered them, and showed them His Father. In spite of their slowness of heart to believe and their many shortcomings Jesus never gave up on them and prepared them to take over His ministry after he departed. The mark of that ministry was obedience to this new commandment "by this all men will know that you are My disciples, if you have love for one another."

As Linda's husband I tried my best to love her as Christ loves His church. That meant rolling up my sleeves to wash dishes every night and descending into the basement to do the laundry every week. They were some of the things that Linda could not do because of a disability. It also meant leading devotions at bedtime every night and praying with her through some trying times. It also meant giving up some of my precious outdoor activities because she was not able to participate in them. But now Linda has departed to a better place and I cannot love her the way I once did. Jesus' command to "love one another" was given to those whom He was leaving behind on this earth. They were to love the others who were left behind. In a similar way we cannot love our departed loved ones the way we used to because they are no longer here with us. There are other family members, friends, and even strangers left in this world that Jesus wants us to concentrate our love on. *"In this is love, not that we loved God, but that He loved us and sent His Son to be the propitiation for our sins. Beloved, if God so loved us, we also ought to love one another. No one has beheld God at any time; if we love one another, God abides in us, and His love is perfected in us."* 1 John 4:10-12. What a wonderful promise, that if we love one another God will abide in us and perfect His love in us. What a blessed way to experience God by giving of ourselves to others. *Therefore be imitators of God, as beloved children; and walk in love, just as Christ also loved you, and gave Himself up for us, an offering and a sacrifice to God as a fragrant aroma, Ephesians 5:1-2.*

Prayer: Dearest Savior; Thank you for the wonderful example of your love. And thank you that you have left others here with us in order for us to love them. Father, heal our hearts and fill us with your love so that we can bless others by helping to meet their needs. Lead us to truly be your body evidenced by your love so that others will be drawn to you. In Jesus name I pray, Amen.

John 13:36; *Simon Peter said to Him, "Lord, where are you going?" Jesus answered, "Where I go, you cannot follow Me now, but you shall follow later."*

On several occasions Jesus told his disciples what was going to happen to Him. One such occasion is recorded in Mark 9:31. *He taught them, "The Son of Man is to be delivered into the hands of men, and they will kill Him; and when He is killed, He will rise three days later."* This prediction comes true as Jesus died on the cross on a Friday and was raised from the tomb three days later on a Sunday. This is a historical fact attested to by the Old Testament Scriptures and many reliable witnesses, most of whom gave their lives for the testimony. Paul writes in I Corinthians 15:3-6, *"For I delivered to you as of first importance what I also received, that Messiah died for our sins according to the Scriptures, and that He was buried, and that He was raised on the third day according to the Scriptures, and that He appeared to Cephas, then to the twelve. After that he appeared to more than five hundred brethren at one time, most of whom remain until now, but some have fallen asleep;"* Not only has Jesus risen from the dead, but because He rose we will be raised also. I Corinthians 15:20-23, *"But now Christ has been raised from the dead, the first fruits of those who are asleep. For since by a man came death, by a man also came the resurrection of the dead. For as in Adam all die, so also in Christ all shall be made alive. But each in his own order: Christ the first fruits, after that those who are Christ's at His coming."* It is a great comfort to know that death is not the end for the child of God because "Messiah has become the first fruits of those who are asleep."

In John 11:21-27 Jesus is confronted by a grieving Martha who had just buried her brother Lazarus.

"Lord, If You had been here, my brother would not have died. Even now I know that whatever You ask of God, God will give You." Jesus said to her, "your brother shall rise again." Martha said to Him, "I know that he will rise again in the resurrection on the last day." Jesus said to her, "I am the resurrection and the life; he who believes in Me shall live even if he dies, and everyone who lives and believes in Me shall never die. Do you believe this?" Jesus is the resurrection and because He has conquered death we also will be resurrected to new life. Therefore we can confidently say with Job, *"And as for me, I know that my Redeemer lives, and at the last He will take His stand on the earth. Even after my skin is destroyed, yet in my flesh I shall see God; whom I myself shall behold, and whom my eyes shall see and not another."* Job 19:25-27. You see dear reader the Bible definitely teaches that there will be a bodily resurrection of the saints of God. These will be bodies free from the devastating effects of sin with no pain, no disease, no aging, no defects, and no death. Some friends of mine have a child who has to spend her whole life in bed and in a wheelchair, but there will come a day when she will be running and jumping, working and playing just like the rest of us even better. No one is immune from the maladies that plague our mortal bodies, but one day *in a flash, in the twinkling of an eye, at the last trumpet. For the trumpet will sound, the dead will be raised imperishable, and we shall be changed. For this perishable must put on the imperishable, and this mortal must put on immortality, 1 Corinthians 15:52-53.*

Prayer: Dear Lord Jesus, Thank you that You have proven Yourself to be the Resurrection by physically rising from the tomb Yourself. And praise You Jesus that You shall return and resurrect our loved ones and change our mortal bodies into ones fit for Heaven. May we live today in the hope and power of Your resurrection. In the name of the ever living One, Jesus, Amen.

Jesus — The Lord of Second Chances, John 13:37-38

John 13:37-38; Peter said to Him, "Lord, why can I not follow You right now? I will lay down my life for Your sake." Jesus answered him, "Will you lay down your life for Me? Truly, truly, I say to you, a cock shall not crow, until you have denied me three times."

When Judas brought the soldiers of the Chief Priests and Pharisees to arrest Jesus, Peter sprang into action to defend Jesus. Peter drew his sword and cut off the ear of the high priest's servant. Jesus quickly intervened, corrected Peter and healed the servant's ear to avert further bloodshed. Jesus was then bound and led away by the soldiers to the residence of the high priest. Peter followed Him into the courtyard. It was there, while Jesus was being beaten and interrogated, that His words were fulfilled and a cold and frightened Peter denied, with cursing, that he knew Jesus three times. *And Peter remembered the word which Jesus had said, "Before a cock crows, you will deny Me three times." And he went out and wept bitterly, Matthew 26:75.* Later, after His resurrection, Jesus approached Peter privately and tenderly restores him to a place of leadership, asking three times, *"Simon son of John, do you love Me?"* and giving him the responsibility, *"Shepherd My sheep".* Peter then goes on to be used of God mightily, preaching the gospel to thousands, performing miracles, becoming a pillar in the early church, and writing two epistles in the Bible; all because Jesus is the Lord of second chances.

Dear reader, do you have regrets in your life? Are there things that you have said or done that may have hurt the loved one that you recently lost? Don't you wish you could go to them to ask for their forgiveness and make things right? Well I have good news for you. Jesus was not only the Lord of second chances for Peter. He is the Lord of second chances for everyone who seeks Him. *If we confess our sins, He is faithful and righteous to forgive us our sins and to cleanse us from all unrighteousness, 1 John 1:9.*

The Lord is compassionate and gracious, slow to anger and abounding in lovingkindness. He will not always strive with us; nor will He keep His anger forever. He has not dealt with us according to our sins, nor rewarded us according to our iniquities. For as high as the heavens are above the earth, so great is His lovingkindness toward those who fear Him. As far as the east is from the west, so far has he removed our transgressions from us. Just as a father has compassion on his children, so the Lord has compassion on those who fear him, Psalm 103:8-13. What a wonderful God we have, not only does He forgive our sins, He also removes them from us. Because Jesus forgives us and commands us to forgive one another, even though your loved one is no longer here but in heaven with Jesus, I believe they will forgive you. Reconciliation is a blessed experience that sets our hearts free to love as God intended. It can never be bound by the grave. We will live forever with Jesus and our loved one without sin and without tears. Why not start right now?

Prayer: Dear Jesus, Thank You for Your unconditional forgiveness which You accomplished for us on the cross. And thank You that my loved one now abides with You in heaven. Lord, help me seek the peace and forgiveness which I need from my loved one. Set my heart free as only You can, Jesus. And thanks for giving me a second chance to love and please You. For Your glory I pray, Amen.

John 14:1; *Let not your heart be troubled; believe in God, believe also in Me.*

Fear can be a debilitating thing, hindering what God wants to do in our lives and stunting our faith. When Moses sent out the twelve spies to spy out the land of Canaan, two of them saw that the land was indeed good, "flowing with milk and honey" and believed that God would make them victorious to take possession of it. However, the other ten spies focused only on the fortified cities and the giant warriors that they had to conquer to obtain the promised land. Fear prevailed and God's plan was delayed for forty years as the children of Israel wandered in the desert. One of the two spies was Joshua who eventually led the children of Israel into the promised land. But God had spoken to him before he went, saying, *"Have I not commanded you? Be strong and courageous! Do not tremble or be dismayed, for the Lord your God is with you wherever you go." Joshua 1:9.* And because God was with Joshua he was able to lead the children of Israel to conquer the land of Canaan.

When your spouse dies, fear and uncertainty can become overwhelming, paralyzing the griever and prolonging the grief period. You may wonder what the future holds or where the money is going to come from to support you and your family. Who is going to be there for you to help you get through life's battles? In order to dispel this fear, Jesus says, *"believe in God, believe also in Me."* He also stated, *"I am the good shepherd; the good shepherd lays down His life for the sheep. But He who enters by the door is the shepherd of the sheep. To Him the doorkeeper opens and the sheep hear his voice, and He calls His own sheep by name, and leads them out. When He puts forth all His own, He goes before them; and the sheep follow Him because they know His voice. I came that they might have life; and might have it abundantly." John10:11, 2-4, 10.* To believe in Jesus means to trust Him completely with your life and follow Him like sheep follow their shepherd. King David was a shepherd himself who protected his sheep from the lion and the bear. He understood what it meant to be under the care of and trust a good shepherd. He wrote, *"The Lord is my shepherd, I shall not want. He makes me lie down in green pastures; He leads me besides quiet waters. He restores my soul; He guides me in the paths of righteousness for His name's sake. Even though I walk through the valley of the shadow of death, I fear no evil; for Thou art with me; Thy rod and Thy staff, they comfort me. Thou dost prepare a table before me in the presence of my enemies; Thou hast anointed my head with oil; My cup overflows. Surely goodness and lovingkindness will follow me all the days of my life, and I will dwell in the house of the Lord forever." Psalm 23.* Dear reader, Jesus being the Good Shepherd means that He will be with you through all of life's troubles, protecting you, providing for you, comforting you, and leading you to eventually dwell in His house forever. His invitation is precious, *Come to Me, all who are weary and heavy-laden, and I will give you rest. Take My yoke upon you, and learn from Me, for I am gentle and humble in heart; and you will find rest for your souls." Matthew11:28-29.*

Prayer: Dear Lord Jesus, many fears tend to flood my soul. Lord I look to you as my Good Shepherd to restore my soul and lead me to quiet waters. I praise You Lord that I can hear Your voice and that You always lead me in paths of righteousness in a chaotic world. I submit to Your yoke as the way to true rest. And I look forward to dwelling in Your house forever, Amen.

John 14:2; *"In My Father's House are many dwelling places; if it were not so, I would have told you; for I go to prepare a place for you."*

Many mighty monarchs throughout history have built for themselves magnificent palaces to dwell in and rule their vast domains from. These colossal castles have many rooms in them for sleeping, dining, playing, dancing, holding court and any activity that the great royal rulers require. They are all lavishly decorated with the most luxurious of fare with no expense being too exorbitant. Today, for a fee, you can tour some of these impressive mansions and dream, like Cinderella, of your prince coming and taking you to his chambers to dwell happily ever after. But all the magnificent palaces constructed by great rulers throughout history pale in comparison to the splendor, majesty, grandeur, beauty, and sheer size of the palace that Jesus calls "My Father's house". It is the dwelling place of the King of kings and Lord of lords where He holds court and rules the universe.

I believe that the place that Jesus refers to as "My Father's house" is described for us in Revelation chapter 21 as "the New Jerusalem." In Revelation 21: 10-14 we read, *And he (an angel) carried me (the Apostle John) away in the Spirit to a great and high mountain and showed me the holy city, Jerusalem, coming down out of heaven from God, having the glory of God. Her brilliance was like a very costly stone, as a stone of crystal-clear jasper.* John goes on to describe a foundation adorned with precious stones, streets of pure gold and gates of pearl. John also gives the dimensions of the city in Revelation 21:16, *And the city is laid out as a square, and its length is as great as the width; and he measured the city with the rod, fifteen hundred miles; its length and width and height are equal.* Randy Alcorn in his book entitled, Heaven, says this about the size of the New Jerusalem; "A metropolis of this size in the middle of the United States would stretch from Canada to Mexico and from the Appalachian Mountains to the California border. The New Jerusalem is all the square footage anyone could ask for. The ground level of the city will be nearly two million square miles. The home of God's people will be extremely large and roomy." Heaven, page 242. If we counted all the followers of Jesus from Pentecost to the end of the Church Age, it could be in the billions. A house the size of the New Jerusalem could easily accommodate them. What a wonderful place Jesus our Bridegroom is preparing for His bride the church. *And I saw the holy city, New Jerusalem, coming down out of heaven from God, made ready as a bride adorned for her husband. And I heard a loud voice from the throne saying, "Behold, the tabernacle of God is among men, and He shall dwell among them, and they shall be His people, and God Himself shall be among them, and He shall wipe away every tear from their eyes; and there shall no longer be any death; there shall no longer be any mourning, or crying, or pain; the first things have passed away."*

And He who sits on the throne said, "Behold, I am making all things new". Revelation 21:2-5.

Prayer: Lord Jesus; Thank you for the precious promise that You are preparing a place for us in Your Father's house. We look forward to the day when we will dwell with You there in the New Jerusalem, a place with no tears, no mourning, pain or death. Praise You Jesus for the glorious resting place where You will dwell forever with Your people. The home You are preparing for us is a wonderful reflection of Your great love for us. "Worthy art Thou, our Lord and our God, to receive glory and honor and power," Amen.

John 14:3; *"And if I go and prepare a place for you, I will come again, and receive you to Myself; that where I am, there you may be also."*

A radio preacher in the area where I live has three times predicted the exact date of the second coming of Jesus Messiah. All three dates have come and gone while Jesus remains in Heaven, disappointing the preacher's listeners and damaging his credibility. Like the boy who cried wolf no one believes him anymore. Fortunately for all true disciples of Jesus we have a promise maker who is a man of perfect integrity. Not only that, Jesus is also God who cannot lie. *"In the same way God, desiring even more to show to the heirs of the promise the unchangeableness of His purpose, interposed with an oath, in order that by two unchangeable things, in which it is impossible for God to lie, we may have strong encouragement, we who fled for refuge in laying hold of the hope set before us. This hope we have as an anchor of the soul, a hope both sure and steadfast and one which enters within the veil, where Jesus has entered as a forerunner for us, having become a high priest forever according to the order of Melchizedek, Hebrews 6:17-20.* Not only can Jesus be completely trusted as a promise giver, He has already predicted several significant events in history that have come to pass exactly the way He said they would. Jesus prophesied His arrest, His crucifixion, His resurrection, His ascension into Heaven, the outpouring of the Holy Spirit on Pentecost, and the destruction of the Temple in Jerusalem. All these events took place just as HE said they would. So there is no reason to ever doubt that when Jesus says, *"I will come again, and receive you to Myself"*, that we will see Him again.

In I Thessalonians 4:14-17 God reveals what will take place on the day of Christ's return for His bride. *"For if we believe that Jesus died and rose again, even so God will bring with Him those who have fallen asleep in Jesus. For this we say to you by the word of the Lord, that we who are alive, and remain until the coming of the Lord, shall not precede those who have fallen asleep. For the Lord Himself will descend from Heaven with a shout, with the voice of the archangel, and with the trumpet of God; and the dead in Christ shall rise first. Then we who are alive and remain shall be caught up together with them in the air, and thus we shall always be with the Lord"*. Everyone who has ever "fallen asleep in Jesus" will come back with Him when He returns. We "shall be caught up together with them in the clouds". What an incredibly joyous reunion that will be when we see Jesus and all our departed loved ones who know Him again!

When we married, Linda and I promised to be together until death do us part. Linda went home to be with Jesus on July 24, 2009. The next time I see Linda it will be forever. "And thus we shall always be with the Lord." What a hope we have! Eternity with our Savior.

"For I consider that the sufferings of this present time are not worthy to be compared with the glory that is to be revealed to us. And not only this, but also we ourselves, having the first fruits of the Spirit, even we ourselves groan within ourselves, waiting eagerly for our adoption as sons, the redemption of our body. For in hope we have been saved, but hope that is seen is not hope; for why does one also hope for what he sees. But if we hope for what we do not see, with perseverance we wait eagerly for it." Romans 8:18, 23-25.

Prayer: Precious Lord Jesus; Thank you for the precious promise of the day that You will return for us. And praise You Lord Jesus that our loved ones will be coming with You! "And Lord, haste the day when the faith shall be sight."- From the hymn It is Well With My Soul by Horatio G. Spafford. In Jesus' precious name we pray, Amen.

John 14:4-6; *"And you know the way where I am going."* Thomas said to Him, *"Lord, we do not know where You are going, how do we know the way?"* Jesus said to him, *"I am the way, and the truth, and the life; no one comes to the Father, but through Me."*

If you have ever watched the classic movie the Wizard of Oz, you might recall the scene where Dorothy is merrily skipping down the Yellow Brick Road, when she comes to a fork in the road. She is faced with the dilemma. Which way should she go? She consults a brainless scarecrow, who was perched there. He crosses his arms and points in both directions. The common popular teaching of this world today is that there are many ways to God. Many influential people say that each of man's religions presents a different path to God. We see bumper stickers with the symbols of the world's major religions and the word "Coexist" on them. This is contrary to the teachings of the Bible and Jesus in particular. He warned, *"Enter by the narrow gate; for the gate is wide, and the way is broad that leads to destruction, and many are those who enter by it. For the gate is small, and the way is narrow that leads to life, and few are those who find it. Beware of the false prophets, who come to you in sheep's clothing, but inwardly are ravenous wolves."* Matthew 7:13-15. Thank God that Jesus is not like the scarecrow pointing in more than one direction or like the false prophets who point in many directions. Fortunately for those of us and our loved ones who have chosen the narrow way, Jesus has made the way to the Father both clear and sure.

In Acts 4:10-12, Peter in order to explain a miraculous healing proclaims, *"let it be known to all of you, and to all the people of Israel, that by the name of Jesus Messiah the Nazarene, whom you crucified, whom God raised from the dead – by this name this man stands before you in good health. He is the stone which was rejected by you, the builders, but which became the very cornerstone. And there is salvation in no one else; for there is no other name under heaven that has been given among men, by which we must be saved."* We can be assured that our loved ones who trusted in the name of Jesus for their salvation are resting in Heaven with Him right now and that we can choose to follow the same Savior who assures us that he is the way to the Father. In 1Timothy 2:3-6 we read, *"This is good and acceptable in the sight of God our Savior, who desires all men to be saved and to come to the knowledge of the truth. For there is one God, and one mediator also between God and men, the man Christ Jesus, who gave Himself as a ransom for all, the testimony borne at the proper time".* Paul encourages us to pray for all men, so that they can be saved and come to the knowledge of the truth and find the right way to the Father. The invitation of Jesus still stands as a beacon to the lost souls of this world, *"I am the bread of life; he who comes to me shall not hunger, and he who believes in Me shall never thirst. For this is the will of My Father, that everyone who beholds the Son and believes in Him, may have eternal life; and I Myself will raise him up on the last day."* John 6:35, 40.

Prayer: Gracious Lord Jesus; Thank you for being the way to the Father and that we can completely put our trust in You that You will get us there. Thank You for being the truth so that we can avoid the lies of this world that lead to destruction. And thank You for being the life that we will enjoy with You and our loved ones forever. In Jesus' name, Amen.

John 14:7-9 *"If you had known Me, you would have known My Father also; from now on you know Him, and have seen Him." Philip said to Him, "Lord show us the Father, and it is enough for us." Jesus said to him, "Have I been so long with you, and yet you have not come to know Me, Philip? He who has seen Me has seen the Father; How do you say show us the Father?"*

Working at a humungous department store I often encounter little children who get separated from their parents. When I hear their desperate cries, "Mommy! Daddy!", I know that I need to locate their parents immediately. In a sense these little ones are saying "show us the father". I can try anything to comfort them, but nothing else will do. They need mommy or daddy. When we lose a close loved one, like a spouse or a parent, we may feel like a little lost child, disoriented and frightened. As His disciples we are all adopted children of the Father of Jesus. *For you are all sons of God through faith in Christ Jesus. For all of you who were baptized into Christ have clothed yourselves with Christ. And because you are sons, God has sent forth the Spirit of His Son into our hearts, crying "Abba! Father!" Galatians 3:26-27; 4:6.* As adopted children of the Father we may sometimes feel forsaken and separated from Him. But we can always cry out, "Abba! Father!", and know that He will come running for us. He will take us into His huge arms and make everything right, comforting us and calming our fears. *The eyes of the Lord are toward the righteous. And his ears are open to their cry. The righteous cry and the Lord hears, and delivers them out of all their troubles. The Lord is near to the brokenhearted, and saves those who are crushed in spirit, Psalm 34:15,17,18.* When our hearts are broken and our spirits are crushed, which happens most when we lose someone close to us, it is an incredible blessing to know that the Lord is near. Our Lord gives special care to those who have lost parents or spouses. *A Father to the fatherless and a judge for the widows, is God in His holy habitation. God makes a home for the lonely, Psalm 68:5-6.*

During His earthly ministry Jesus constantly demonstrated His compassion for the broken and unfortunate souls which He encountered. *And Jesus was going about all the cities and the villages, teaching in their synagogues, and proclaiming the gospel of the kingdom, and healing every kind of disease and every kind of sickness. And seeing the multitudes, He felt compassion for them, because they were distressed and downcast like sheep without a shepherd, Matthew 9:35-36.* The heart of Jesus is a heart of compassion for the distressed and downcast. Jesus not only felt for them He also used His power as the Son of God to change the condition of their lives. *Now when John in prison heard of the works of Christ, he sent word by his disciples, and said to Him, "Are You the Expected One, or shall we look for someone else?" And Jesus answered and said to them, "Go and report to John what you hear and see: the blind receive sight and the lame walk, the lepers are cleansed and the deaf hear, and the dead are raised up, and the poor have the gospel preached to them," Matthew 11:2-5.* Like Father, like Son, the works that Jesus did here on earth show us the Father. *"Truly, truly, I say to you, the Son can do nothing of Himself, unless it is something He sees the Father doing; for whatever the Father does, these things the Son does in like manner. For the Father loves the Son, and shows Him all things that He Himself is doing; and greater works than these will He show Him, that you may marvel." John 5:19-20.*

Prayer: Dear Jesus, Thank you for showing us the heart and nature of Your Father. And thank You that when we are crushed and brokenhearted You are near to us. In your holy name I pray, Amen.

John 14:10-11 *"Do you not believe that I am in the Father, and the Father is in Me? The words that I say to you I do not speak on My own initiative, but the Father abiding in Me does his works. Believe Me that I am in the Father, and the Father in Me, otherwise believe on account of the works themselves."*

"Married-Filing Jointly", tears welled up in my eyes as I checked this box for the last time. On our wedding day Linda and I had these verses read in our service: *"But from the beginning of creation, God made them male and female. For this cause a man shall leave his father and mother, and the two shall become one flesh; consequently they are no longer two, but one flesh." Mark 10:6-8.* We did our best to live out the experience of being "one flesh". We always lived in the same home, maintained the same budget, and went to one church. We taught Sunday school together, made decisions together, and raised our daughter together. But then the unthinkable happened. I woke up one morning and Linda had unexpectedly left her body. There was nothing but an empty shell lying next to me in bed. I frantically tried to bring her back, but she was in a better place with Jesus, and I do not think she would have returned even if she could. Finally I yielded to the inevitable and God's will was done.

Jesus' disciples had witnessed all the works of Jesus, every healing, every demon cast out, waves stilled, water turned to wine and the dead raised back to life to name a few. *Many other signs therefore Jesus also performed in the presence of the disciples, which are not written in this book; but these have been written that you may believe that Jesus is the Christ, the Son of God; and that believing you may have life in His name, John 20:30-31.* Then the unthinkable happened. The Messiah, that they had put their hope in was arrested, tried, and executed on a cruel Roman cross. The promise of God from the ancient Scriptures seemed to go unfulfilled. All hope for Messiah's kingdom seemed lost as "the King of the Jews" hung between two thieves. Jesus cried out, *"My God, My God, why hast Thou forsaken Me"*, and then, *"it is finished"* and yielded up His spirit. But what exactly did Jesus mean when He said "it is finished." What He meant was that the Father's plan for the redemption of lost mankind was accomplished. Peter proclaimed, *"Men of Israel, listen to these words; Jesus the Nazarene, a man attested to you by God with miracles and wonders and signs which God performed through Him in your midst, just as you yourselves know- this Man, delivered up by the predetermined plan and foreknowledge of God, you nailed to a cross by the hands of godless men and put Him to death."Acts 2:22-23.* The Messiah hanging on the cross was part of God's "predetermined plan" and Jesus sacrificed His life in obedience to the will of His Father. Our redemption was not only preplanned, it was also promised and prophesied in Scripture. Isaiah proclaimed, *"All of us like sheep have gone astray, each has turned to his own way; but the Lord has caused the iniquity of us all to fall on Him. But the Lord was pleased to crush Him, putting Him to grief; if He would render Himself as a guilt offering. As a result of the anguish of His soul, He will see it and be satisfied; by His knowledge the Righteous One, My Servant, will justify the many, as He will bear their iniquities." Isaiah 53:6, 10, 11. You were not redeemed with perishable things like silver or gold from your futile way of life inherited from your forefathers, but with precious blood, as of a lamb unblemished and spotless, the blood of Christ, 1Peter 1:18-19.*

Prayer: Father thank you that You and Jesus are one in every way. And thank you in particularly for being one in the plan and accomplishment of our redemption. Praise You, Lamb of God who takes away our sin and brings us all home. Amen.

John 14:13-14 *"And whatever you ask in My name, that I will do, that the Father may be glorified in the Son. If you ask anything in My name, I will do it."*

My wife Linda had a skin disease in her feet that caused them to dry out, crack, and itch irritatingly. She needed a medicinal cream applied to them every night. Her cry would always be, "Honey, can you rub my feet?" I would answer by massaging the cream into her sore and itching feet because I loved her and was concerned for her comfort and well-being. This usually led to a most intimate and wonderful time of fellowship with each other.

Jesus appeals to our hurting souls in Revelation 3:20 when He says, *"Behold, I stand at the door and knock; if anyone hears my voice and opens the door, I will come in to him, and will dine with him, and he with Me."* In the little church where I grew up there hangs on the wall behind the pulpit a large portrait of Jesus standing outside of a door knocking to come in. The door in the picture purposely has no door knob on the outside. When I asked about it the pastor said it's because Jesus won't force His way into our hearts, we must open from within to give Him access. Jesus knows the mess that we are. He sees our hurt and sorrow, our sin and distress. Jesus has what it takes to bring relief from whatever this world afflicts us with. He knocks sometimes quietly, sometimes more urgently. To pray is to open that door and give Him full access to our hearts. He promises, *"whatever you ask in My name, that I will do."* An old Norwegian bible teacher, O. Hallesby, defines prayer in his book entitled "Prayer"; "To pray is nothing more involved than to let Jesus into our needs. To pray is to give Jesus permission to employ His powers in the alleviation of our distress. To pray is to let Jesus glorify His name in the midst of our needs. God has designed prayer as a means of intimate and joyous fellowship between God and man." To pray is to sit down and sup with Jesus. *"Indeed our fellowship is with the Father, and with His Son Jesus Christ."* 1 John 1:3. What a blessed privilege. God has given us access to our greatest need, Jesus Himself. *Now as they were travelling along, He entered a certain village, and a woman named Martha welcomed Him to her home. And she had a sister called Mary, who moreover was listening to the Lord's word, seated at His feet. But Martha was distracted with all her preparations; and she came up to Him, and said, "Lord, do you not care that my sister has left me to do all the serving alone? Then tell her to help me." But the Lord answered and said to her, "Martha, Martha, you are worried and bothered about so many things; but only a few things are necessary, really only one, for Mary has chosen the good part, which shall not be taken away from her,"* Luke 10:38-42. Reader, reader, are you worried and bothered about many things? Sit down and take some time to choose the good part, which shall not be taken away from you. This is what Jesus wants from us more than anything else, our wholehearted devotion. He knows what is best for us. What a friend we have in Jesus, all our sins and griefs to bear! What a privilege to carry everything to God in prayer! – Joseph M. Scriven. Jesus may have gone to His Father's house in heaven, but He is always just a prayer away. *"Cease striving (or be still) and know that I am God"*, Psalm 46:10.

Prayer: Thank you precious Savior that You are always available for us to commune with in prayer. Thank you that You are "able to do exceeding abundantly beyond all that we ask or think", Ephesians 3:20. Lord Jesus You are the answer to our most pressing need. Thank You Jesus that there is blessed peace found at your feet and like Mary we choose "the good part". Amen.

John 14:15 *"If you love Me, you will keep My commandments."*

Loving God and keeping His commandments is nothing new. Moses, when he was preparing the children of Israel to enter the promised land shared God's requirements for righteous living there. In Deuteronomy 10:12-13 Moses says, *"And now, Israel, what does the Lord your God require from you, but to fear the Lord your God, to walk in His ways and love Him, and to serve the Lord your God with all your heart and with all your soul, and to keep the Lord's commandments and His statutes which I am commanding you today for your good?"* The children of Israel were to have a love relationship with the Lord their God evidenced by their serving Him and obeying His commandments. When you love someone in authority over you it is much more enjoyable, desirable and profitable to obey their commandments. Those who love God also love His word and enjoy living their lives according to His commandments. Psalm 119 is all about the joy and blessing of keeping God's commandments. Here are a few verses from the longest Psalm in the Bible. *Give me understanding, that I may observe Thy law, and keep it with all my heart. Make me walk in the path of Thy commandments, for I delight in it. Psalm 119:34-35.* Jesus raises the standard for righteous living for those who would love and follow Him. He said, *"Unless your righteousness surpasses that of the scribes and Pharisees, you shall not enter the kingdom of heaven,"* Matthew 5:20. As disciples of Jesus we are to bless those who persecute and slander us, not get angry with our brother, but to reconcile with him and forgive him seventy times seven, not lust with our eyes, not divorce our mates, turn the other cheek, love our enemies and make disciples of all nations to name a few. According to Jesus the life of His disciples is more demanding than the life of the children of Israel who follow Moses. It is only by His grace and power within us that makes us able to obey and love Jesus in a way that transforms our world and gains us access into His kingdom.

When I think of disciples who really love Jesus and show it by their faithful obedience to Him, I think of my friends, John and Cheryl Daily. When my family moved it took longer than anticipated John stayed behind to finish unloading the truck when everyone else had to leave. John went the extra miles for us because he was a brother who really loved Jesus. When Jesus called John and Cheryl to go to France to plant churches, they endured a long deputation, packed up their three children with all their belongings and moved to what is referred to as the graveyard of missionaries. Together they faced the challenge of winning their resistant French neighbors to Messiah until one dark December night when John lost his life in a car accident while serving Jesus. Cheryl courageously stayed the course despite her loss and continues to serve Jesus as a widowed missionary in France, because she loves Him and wants to obey Him no matter what happens. She and her three children are still there manifesting the love of Jesus to everyone they meet, making disciples as Jesus has commanded them. *Whoever believes that Jesus is the Christ is born of God; and whoever loves the Father loves the child born of Him. By this we know that we love the children of God, when we love God and observe His commandments. For this is the love of God, that we keep His commandments; and His commandments are not burdensome, 1 John 5:1-3.*

Prayer: Dear Lord; My rebel soul finds it difficult at times to obey you. Please forgive my disobedience and thank You for being obedient unto death on a cross for me. Restore in me a heart of love for You, Jesus. And a delight to obey Your Word that I may know the joy of a life given over to You. Amen.

John 14:16-17 *"And I will ask the Father, and He will give you another Helper, that He may be with you forever; that is the Spirit of truth, whom the world cannot receive, because it does not behold Him or know Him, but you know Him because He abides with you, and will be in you."*

Jesus gives us this most precious promise, "Another Helper," Parakletos in the original Greek, which means One who comes alongside to help. The picture is like one of a wounded soldier fallen in battle, unable to get himself up to walk to safety. A fellow soldier comes along side of him, picks him up and holding him upright walks him away from the battleground to safety. In our battle with grief and sin we often fall and find ourselves powerless to overcome and get ourselves back on the right road. But Jesus provides salvation. He does this by sending "another Helper", "the Spirit of truth" to save us from sin; give us new life and the power to overcome. *"He saved us, not on the basis of deeds which we have done in righteousness, but according to His mercy, by the washing of regeneration and renewing by the Holy Spirit, Whom He poured out upon us richly through Jesus Christ our Savior," Titus 3:5-6.*

Sometimes, and particularly when we suffer through seasons of grief, we find ourselves so weak and disoriented that we are unable to pray. At those times God the Holy Spirit intercedes for us from within our own hearts. *"And in the same way the Spirit also helps our weakness; for we do not know how to pray as we should, but the Spirit himself intercedes for us with groaning too deep for words, and He who searches the hearts knows what the mind of Spirit is, because He intercedes for the saints according to the will of God," Romans 8:26-27.* What a comfort and a blessing it is to have God the Holy Spirit dwelling within us, giving us peace and lifting us up when we are down. When someone that we are close with dies in many ways we tend to die with them. Depression and grief weigh us down and make us feel dead inside. Praise God that He is in the resurrection and restoration business. *Then He said to me, "Prophesy to the breath, prophesy, son of man, and say to the breath, Thus says the Lord God, Come from the four winds, O breath, and breathe on these slain, that they come to life." So I prophesied as He commanded me, and the breath came into them, and they came to life, and stood on their feet, an exceedingly great army. And I will put My Spirit within you, and you will come to life. Ezekiel 37:9-10, 14.*

As God picked up dust from the earth and breathed on it and created Adam and gave him life, He will also breathe on this dust, that is our bodies and souls, with His Holy Spirit and give us new life. *"But if the Spirit of Him who raised Jesus from the dead dwells in you, He who raised Christ Jesus from the dead will also give life to your mortal bodies through His Spirit who indwells you," Romans 8:11.* The gift of the Holy Spirit is given to all those who choose to believe in Jesus. Jesus Himself promised, *"If any man is thirsty, let him come to Me and drink. He who believes in Me, as the Scripture said, from his innermost being shall flow rivers of living water. But this He spoke of the Spirit, whom those who believed in Him were to receive." John 7:37-39.*

Prayer: Lord Jesus; Thank you for sending "another Helper" on the day that I first believed in You. Holy Spirit thank you that You are living in me, renewing me, resurrecting me, carrying me, and interceding for me especially during my times of weakness. Praise You Lord Jesus for "the rivers of living water" ever flowing from my "innermost being". Amen.

John 14:18 *"I will not leave you as orphans; I will come to you."*

What do you suppose it would be like to be an orphan, a child with no father or mother? No one to care for you, love you, feed you, protect you, and provide shelter for you. In Psalm 109:9, 10, &12 God says of the wicked; *"let his children be fatherless, and his wife a widow. Let his children wander about and beg; and let them seek sustenance far from their ruined homes. Let there be none to extend lovingkindness to him, nor to be gracious to his fatherless children."* It's a horrible picture, but one that is all too common in this cruel fallen world where sin, death, disease and war leave many children destitute, without caregivers. Fortunately for them; *"A Father to the fatherless and a judge for the widows, is God in His holy habitation,"* Psalm 68:5.

To His disciples Jesus was everything. Peter said to Jesus; *"Behold we have left everything and followed You;"* and *"Lord, to whom shall we go? You have the words of eternal life"*, Matthew 19:27, John 6:68. Now Jesus was going to the cross to die, leaving them like orphans. His promise, "I will come to you" will be fulfilled on three different occasions and in three different ways. First, Jesus physically appeared to his disciples several times after his resurrection. One time is recorded in John 20:26-29; *And after eight days again His disciples were inside, and Thomas with them. Jesus came, the doors having been shut, and stood in their midst, and said, "Peace be with you." Then he said to Thomas, "Reach here your finger, and see My hands; reach here your hand, and put it into My side; and be not unbelieving, but believing." Thomas answered and said to Him, "My Lord and my God!" Jesus said to him, "Because you have seen Me, have you believed? Blessed are they who did not see, and yet believed."* Jesus appeared to minister peace to His mourning disciples and faith to a doubting Thomas.

The second way Jesus was going to visit them was through the outpouring of His Holy Spirit. In Acts 1:4-5, 8 Jesus appears to them again and gives them directions and this promise; *And gathering them together, He commanded them not to leave Jerusalem, but to wait for what the Father had promised, "Which," He said, "you heard of from Me; for John baptized with water, but you shall be baptized with the Holy Spirit not many days from now. But you shall receive power when the Holy Spirit has come upon you; and you shall be My witnesses both in Jerusalem, and in all Judea and Samaria, and even to the remotest part of the earth."* The rest of the book of Acts and church history tells the story of the visitation of God the Holy Spirit upon the followers of Jesus and the wonders that He has accomplished, is accomplishing and will yet accomplish.

The third return of Jesus is yet future and is called the blessed hope of the church. We read in Acts 1:10-11, *And as they were gazing intently into the sky while He was departing, behold, two men in white clothing stood beside them; and they also said, "Men of Galilee, why do you stand looking into the sky? This Jesus, who has been taken up from you into heaven, will come in just the same way as you have watched Him go into heaven."* The promise of Jesus for His followers is that, *"I will not leave you as orphans; I will come to you."* Hallelujah! Jesus has fulfilled this promise twice and we can be assured that He will come back for us and will vindicate all the injustices done on this earth.

Prayer: Thank you Jesus that we are not left as orphans. And that You are alive and live in us. And thank you for the blessed hope that we have in Your physical return to take us home to be with You forever. Maranatha! Come quickly Lord! Amen.

John 14:19 *"After a little while the world will behold me no more; but you will behold Me; because I live, you shall live also."*

Time is running out for this old world. Soon they will behold Jesus no more. The age of God's grace is going to come to an end. The door of the Ark is soon to be closed and the darkness of judgment will descend like rain. *Jesus therefore said, "For a little while longer I am with you, then I go to Him who sent me. You shall seek Me, and shall not find Me; and where I am, you cannot come," John 7:33-34. He said therefore again to them, "I go away, and you shall seek Me, and shall die in your sin; where I am going you cannot come. You are from below, I am from above; you are of this world, I am not of this world. I said therefore to you, that you shall die in your sins; for unless you believe that I am He, you shall die in your sins." John 8:21, 23-24.* What an awful thought, eternity without Messiah. But it does not have to be this way for anyone. The invitation is still open. Jesus is Jehovah, the "I am" of Exodus 3:14. Faith in Him is essential for eternal life. *"Truly, truly, I say to you, he who hears my word, and believes Him who sent me, has eternal life, and does not come into judgment, but has passed out of death into life. Truly, truly, I say to you, an hour is coming and now is, when the dead shall hear the voice of the Son of God; and those who hear shall live. For just as the Father has life in Himself, even so He gave to the Son also to have life in Himself, and He gave him authority to execute judgment, because He is the Son of Man. Do not marvel at this, for an hour is coming, in which all who are in the tombs shall hear His voice, and shall come forth, those who did good deeds to a resurrection of life, those who committed the evil deeds to a resurrection of judgment." John 5:24-29.* As Jesus commanded Lazarus to come forth from his tomb, He will speak once more and all the dead shall hear His voice and come forth. For the believer it will be a resurrection to eternal life, but for those who reject Messiah it will be a terrible resurrection to eternal death in hell.

The one who believes in the Son of God has the witness in himself, the one who does not believe God has made Him a liar, because he has not believed in the witness that God has borne concerning His Son. And the witness is this that God has given us eternal life, and this life is in His Son. He who has the Son has the life; he who does not have the Son of God does not have the life. These things I have written to you who believe in the name of the Son of God in order that you may know that you have eternal life, 1 John 5:10-13.

Because Jesus was resurrected and lives He promises, *"You shall also live."* Not only will Messiah live forever, so will those who are His. *But now Christ has been raised from the dead, the first fruits of those who are asleep. For since by a man came death, by a man also came the resurrection of the dead. For as in Adam all die, so also in Christ all shall be made alive. But each in his own order; Christ the first fruits, after that those who are Christ's at His coming, 1 Corinthians 15:20-23.*

Prayer: Dear Jesus, Thank you for the assurance we find in Your words that those who put their faith in You have eternal life. Lord we know that it is not Your will that any should perish. Help us proclaim Your word so that many more souls will pass out of death into life eternal with You. Praise God for Your resurrection and our future resurrection. We look forward to Your coming, Lord Jesus. Amen.

John 14:20 *"In that day you shall know that I am in My Father, and you in Me, and I in you."*

What we have seen and heard we proclaim to you also, that you may have fellowship with us; and indeed our fellowship is with the Father, and with His Son Jesus Christ, 1 John 1:3.

Throughout all eternity God the Father and God the Son have enjoyed a perfect oneness of fellowship.

They are one in essence, both being fully God according to Colossians 1:15, 2:9. *And He (Jesus) is the image of the invisible God, the first-born of all creation. For in Him all the fullness of Deity dwells in bodily form.* Jesus recalls fondly His precreation relationship with His Father while speaking to His Father. *"And now, glorify Thou Me together with Thyself Father, with the glory which I had with Thee before the world was." John 17:5.*

The Father and the Son are also one in word or teaching. *Jesus therefore answered them, and said, "My teaching is not Mine, but His who sent Me." "For I did not speak on My own initiative, but the Father Himself who sent Me has given Me commandment, what to say, and what to speak. And I know that His commandment is eternal life, therefore I speak just as the Father has told me." John 7:16, 12:49-50.*

The Father and Jesus are also unified in will and works. Jesus said, *"For I have come down from heaven, not to do My own will, but the will of Him who sent Me", "For the Father loves the Son, and shows Him all things that He Himself is doing; and greater works than these will He show Him, that you may marvel." "If I do not do the works of My Father, do not believe Me; but if I do them, though you do not believe Me, believe the works, that you may know and understand that the Father is in Me, and I in the Father." John 6:38, 5:20, 10:37-38.* Jesus prayed that we may come to know both the Father and Himself. To Him *"this is eternal life, that they may know Thee, the only true God, and Jesus Christ whom Thou hast sent." John 17:3.* Knowing the only true God and Jesus is what brings us eternal life. In fact the very reason that Jesus died on the cross was to bring us to God. *For Christ also died for sins once for all, the just for the unjust, in order that He might bring us to God. 1 Peter 3:18.*

We are secure in Messiah because we are kept by the Father and the Son. *"And I am no more in the world; yet they themselves are in the world, and I come to Thee, Holy Father, keep them in Thy name, the name which Thou hast given Me, that they may be one, even as We are. While I was with them, I was keeping them in Thy name which Thou hast given Me; and I guarded them, and not one of them perished."* John 17:11-12. God wants His children to experience the same oneness that the Father has with the Son. *"I do not ask in behalf of these alone, but for those also who believe in Me through their word; that they may all be one; even as Thou, Father, art in Me, and I in Thee, that they be in Us; that the world may believe that Thou didst send Me. And the glory which Thou hast given Me I have given to them; that they may be one, just as We are one; I in them, and Thou in Me, that they may be perfected in unity, that the world may know that Thou didst send Me, and didst love them, even as Thou didst love Me." John 17:20-23.*

Prayer: Dear Lord Jesus; Thank You that You have made it possible for us to know You and Your Father. And thank You for the assurance that because we know the one true God and Jesus Messiah that we have eternal life. Praise You Lord Jesus for the oneness that we can have with You and the Father, and the unity that we can enjoy with our fellow siblings in Messiah. For Your glory I pray. Amen.

John 14:21 *"He who has My commandments and keeps them, he it is who loves Me; and he who loves Me shall be loved by My Father, and I will love him, and will disclose Myself to him."*

After His resurrection Jesus commanded His disciples, *"Go therefore and make disciples of all the nations, baptizing them in the name of the Father and the Son and the Holy Spirit, teaching them to observe all I command you;"* Matthew 28:19. Two of Jesus' disciples who obeyed this command were Peter and John. After Jesus had ascended into heaven they were living in Jerusalem. One day they were going to the temple to pray. At the gate of the temple sat a crippled man who could not stand from birth. He was placed there to beg alms from the good people who entered the temple, because there were no disability checks back then and this was the only way he could survive. Peter went up to him and said, *"I do not possess silver or gold, but what I have I give to you: In the name of Jesus Christ the Nazarene – walk! And seizing him by the right hand, he raised him up; and immediately his feet and his ankles were strengthened. And with a leap, he stood upright and began to walk; and he entered the temple with them, walking and leaping and praising God. And all the people saw him walking and praising God; and they were taking note of him as being the one who used to sit at the Beautiful Gate of the temple to beg alms, and they were filled with wonder and amazement at what had happened to him."* Acts 3:6-10. Peter was forced to preach a sermon to explain what Jesus had done for this once crippled man. He told the people that it was Jesus whom they disowned before Pilate that healed this man. He told them that the prophets had foretold the sufferings of God's Messiah. Peter then commanded them, *"Repent therefore and return, that your sins may be wiped away, in order that times of refreshing may come from the Lord; and that He may send Jesus, the Christ appointed for you,"* Acts 3:19-20. The result was that many heard the message and 5,000 men, not including women and children, believed and returned to the Lord that day. All because two of Jesus' disciples loved Him and obeyed just one of His commandments.

What a precious fellowship we have with a Heavenly Father and a Savior who loves us. We are never alone and never without hope and comfort. It was wonderful being married for almost 11 years. My wife Linda was an incredible woman and I enjoyed learning about her every day we were together. In our close intimate relationship we were free to disclose our innermost thoughts, feelings and dreams with each other. I sure do miss her now, but Jesus is more than capable to bless my soul. Linda's loss has brought a wonderful opportunity to become more intimately acquainted with my Savior as He discloses more of Himself to me every day.

Prayer: Thank you Jesus for the testimony of Peter and John. How they obeyed Your commandment and witnessed Your love poured out on more than 5,000 people. Thank You Lord for Your promise to love us and bless us when we obey Your word. May You Lord Jesus be glorified in our lives as we obey You and bask in the love of Your Father and Yourself. Amen.

John 14:23 *"If anyone loves Me, he will keep My word; and My Father will love him, and We will come to him and make Our abode with him."*

In the first of the Ten Commandments God says this; *"You shall have no other gods before Me. You shall not make for yourselves an idol, or any likeness of what is in heaven above or on earth beneath or in the water under the earth. You shall not worship them or serve them; for I, the LORD your God, am a jealous God, visiting the iniquity of the fathers on the children, on the third and fourth generations of those who hate Me, but showing lovingkindness to thousands, to those who love Me and keep My commandments." Exodus 20:3-6.*

In the Prophecy of Daniel three young Jewish men, Shadrach, Meshach, and Abed-Nego, were living in exile in Babylon and served as governors under King Nebuchadnezzar. The king set up a huge image of gold and commanded all his subjects to bow down and worship it or be thrown into a fiery furnace. But these three Jewish men loved their God and refused to bow down to Nebuchadnezzar's golden image. When the enraged king threatened to throw them into the furnace of blazing fire they replied, *"Our God whom we serve is able to deliver us from the furnace of blazing fire; and He will deliver us out of your hand, O king. But even if He does not, let it be made known to you, O king, that we are not going to serve your gods or worship the golden image that you have set up." Daniel 3:17-18.* King Nebuchadnezzar got even more enraged and had them bound and cast into the furnace of blazing fire. When the king looked into the furnace he was amazed at what he saw. *He answered and said, "Look! I see four men loosed and walking about in the midst of the fire without harm, and the appearance of the fourth is like a son of the gods!" Daniel 3:25.* It is believed by many Bible scholars that the fourth man in the fire with Shadrach, Meshach, and Abed-Nego, was Jesus, the Son of the only God Himself. We know that Jesus promises to love and abide with those who love and obey Him. He will do this especially when we are called to go through fiery trials like Shadrach, Meshach, and Abed-Nego.

When I lost my wife, Linda, Jesus was there in the midst of my grief and sorrow. It was Jesus Himself who brought me through unharmed by the fire. And I know that Jesus will be there for you if you love Him and keep His word.

Jesus gives us this invitation in Revelation 3:20-21: *Behold, I stand at the door and knock; if anyone hears My voice and opens the door, I will come into him, and will dine with him, and he with Me. He who overcomes, I will grant to him to sit down with Me on My throne, as I also overcame and sat down with My Father on His throne."*

Prayer: Dear Jesus, Thank You for the promise that You will be with me no matter what trials life may bring my way. You are the Son of God who loves His children when we are faithful and obedient. Lord I love You and will not bow to anyone's idol and trust You to give me strength as I choose to stand for You, Jesus. Amen.

John 14:26 *"But the Helper, the Holy Spirit, whom the Father will send in My name, He will teach you all things, and bring to your remembrance all that I said to you."*

The Gospel of John is an amazing book. My copy is a red letter edition where the words of Jesus are printed in red ink. But according to church history John did not write down his gospel until about fifty years after Jesus had left this planet. How did the apostle manage to remember the exact words of Jesus after fifty years? The answer is found in the words of Jesus in John 14:26, *"the Holy Spirit will teach you all things, and bring to your remembrance all that I said to you."* God's word is a wonderful blessing to those who treasure it in their hearts. *"Thy word I have treasured in my heart, that I may not sin against Thee,"* Psalm 119:11. As children our memories were sharp and if we were taught to memorize Bible verses what a treasure we possessed, even though we may have despised the exercise. But I have learned that the older we get the duller our minds become and remembering things is not as easy as it once was. But praise the name of Jesus that we have been given His memory Helper who abides within us, and who brings to mind precious Scriptures that are just the words we need at just the right times. *"A man has joy in an apt answer, and how delightful is a timely word!" Proverbs 15:23.*

When someone loses a loved one it is difficult to know what to say to comfort them. God's word is full of wonderful words of faith and peace that minister to hurting souls. But which verses should I use and how can I remember them? A quick prayer to our inner Helper can bring to mind what God wants us to share at any given moment. Even in times of distress and trouble the Holy Spirit is there to help us in our time of need. *"But when they deliver you up, do not be anxious about how or what you will speak; for it shall be given you in that hour what you are to speak. For it is not you who speak, but it is the Spirit of your Father who speaks in you," Matthew 10:19-20.* What a blessing we have in God the Holy Spirit. Jesus has promised, *"He who believes in Me, as the Scripture said, 'From his inner-most being shall flow rivers of living water.' But this He spoke of the Holy Spirit, whom those who believed in Him were to receive;" John 7:38-39.* What a blessing we have inside. Like Jesus we can be a fountain of living water able to refresh thirsty souls.

"'For My thoughts are not your thoughts, Neither are your ways My ways,' declares the LORD. 'For as the heavens are higher than the earth, So are My ways higher than your ways, And My thoughts higher than your thoughts. For as the rain and the snow come down from heaven, and do not return there without watering the earth, And making it bear and sprout, And furnishing seed to the sower and bread to the eater; So shall My word be which goes forth from My mouth; It shall not return to Me empty, Without accomplishing what I desire, And without succeeding in the matter for which I sent it. For you will go out with joy, And be led forth with peace;' " Isaiah 55:8-12.

Prayer: Dear Lord Jesus, We often fail to find the right words to say when someone is in need. Thank You for the presence of Your Holy Spirit in our hearts. May we have ears attentive to His leading and minds filled with the treasure of Your word. May we be fountains of Your living water to the thirsty souls around us. For Your glory we pray, Amen.

John 14:27 *"Peace I leave with you, My peace I give to you; not as the world gives, do I give to you. Let not your heart be troubled, nor let it be fearful."*

Shalom! Shalom in Hebrew means peace. It is used by Jewish people as a greeting to wish peace and wellbeing to friends and family. Unfortunately peace for our Jewish friends has been elusive in this world. Troubled souls throughout this world vainly seek for peace. When the horrors of death take its toll those who are left behind struggle to find peace of mind. Many suffer sleepless nights as their distraught souls cry out for relief.

Fortunately, there is a man who is full of peace because He is the Prince of Peace. When Jesus was born and became flesh the angels in Heaven proclaimed, *"Glory to God in the highest, And on earth peace among men, with whom He is pleased." Luke 2:14.* Hallelujah! Peace has come to a peaceless world. Because Jesus brings peace to troubled souls. The Apostle Paul says in Romans 5:1, *"We have peace with God through our Lord Jesus Christ"* How did Jesus accomplish this peace? Paul goes on to say in Romans 5:8, *"God demonstrates His own love toward us, in that while we were yet sinners, Christ died for us."* You see our sin had made a separation between us and God. There exists an impassable chasm, like the Grand Canyon, between sinful man and a Holy God. But the good news is that Messiah has died to remove our sin and bring us across that chasm to be reconciled to His Father. By His sacrifice Jesus became our peace and imparts to us His eternal inner peace. My friends, do you have peace with God through the Lord Jesus Messiah? Have you by faith received the peace that only comes from knowing God? Jesus has opened the door to Heaven, won't you come in before it's too late?

Ten Jewish men huddled together, hiding in a lonely room with the door shut for fear of the men who crucified Jesus. These men were troubled souls who had just lost their Messiah, whom they had put all their hope and faith in. Suddenly! Out of nowhere, *"Jesus came and stood in their midst, and said to them, 'Peace be with you,' "John 20:19.* Jesus not only spoke peace to those troubled souls, He imparted His peace to them. *"Jesus therefore said to them again, 'Peace be with you; As the Father has sent Me, I also send you.' And when He had said this, He breathed on them, and said to them, 'Receive the Holy Spirit,' "John 20:21-22.*

The peace that Jesus imparted to His ten disciples was not for them only. The peace of Jesus is promised to all believers who call on Him in prayer in the midst of their anxiety.

"Be anxious for nothing, but in everything by prayer and supplication with thanksgiving let your requests be made known to God. And the peace of God, which surpasses all comprehension, shall guard your hearts and your minds in Christ Jesus." Philippians 4:6-7. Whether you have known Jesus for many years or have yet to put your faith in Him, Jesus still offers this precious promise in Matthew 11:28. *"Come to Me, all who are weary and heavy-laden, and I will give you rest."*

Prayer: Precious Lord Jesus, Our hearts are often troubled by the turmoil and strife in the world in which we live. Losing a loved one to death is a crushing blow to our soul. Lord Jesus we desperately need Your peace. Come to us dear Lord and impart Your peace and give us rest. In You precious Jesus we place our faith and hope, forever and ever, Amen.

John 14:28 *"You heard that I said to you, 'I go away, and I will come to you.' If you loved Me, you would have rejoiced, because I go to the Father; for the Father is greater than I."*

I know a couple of young men who come from nice cozy homes and wonderful loving families. They both chose to leave the comfort of their homes to join the Marine Corps and go on missions to the front lines in the war in Afghanistan. They lived in the most uncomfortable of places with the danger of losing their lives a constant threat. What a relief and blessing it will be to them to complete their missions and return home. What a joyful reception they will receive when they are welcomed home with hugs, kisses, tears of joy, and the finest of fare.

Like these young men Jesus left His Father's home above. He was born in a lowly manger, lived mostly by meager means, and sacrificed Himself on a cruel cross for the sins of the world. He accomplished His mission of redeeming the world and now has returned to the glory of His Father's home in Heaven. What a joyful, triumphant, and glorious reception He must have received. Before He departed Jesus told His disciples; *"if you loved Me, you would have rejoiced, because I go to the Father;"* John 14:28.

Recently I have friends who moved from one house to a nicer house. I rejoiced with them as they excitedly showed me their new home. When someone who knows Jesus leaves this old world to go to the Father's house above shouldn't we rejoice even more? Certainly if we truly loved them we would put their well-being above our own feelings and rejoice that they are in a much more wonderful home than the one they had here. My wife Linda was in poor physical condition and suffered much pain during the eleven years that I knew her. Today she is enjoying a new body with no defects, pain or disease. She is able to run, jump, dance and do many things she could not do here with her bad knees and severe case of fibromyalgia.

The Apostle Paul who knew much suffering said, *"For we know that if the earthly tent which is our house is torn down, we have a building from God, a house not made with hands, eternal in the heavens. For indeed in this house we groan, longing to be clothed with our dwelling from heaven;"* 2 Corinthians 5:1-2. Linda groaned much in her "earthly tent" but is thoroughly enjoying her "dwelling from heaven" right now. The Bible teaches us that in Heaven God will, *"wipe away every tear from their eyes; and there shall no longer be any death; there shall no longer be any mourning, or crying, or pain; the first things have passed away. And He who sits on the throne said, 'Behold, I am making all things new;' "* Revelation 21:4-5. "When we all get to Heaven, what a day of rejoicing that will be! When we all see Jesus we'll sing and shout the victory!" – Eliza E. Hewitt.

Prayer: Dear Jesus; We love You and rejoice that You accomplished Your mission of redeeming what was lost and now reside with Your Father in Heaven. Thank You Jesus for Your promise that You will not leave us here, but will come and take us home with You when our mission is completed on this earth. Thank that our loved ones who loved You and completed their missions are now rejoicing in new bodies with You in Your Father's house. What a comfort to know they are with You in glory and that if we trust in You, Jesus, we will be joyfully reunited some sweet day. Even so, come quickly Lord! Amen.

"I am the true vine, and My Father is the vinedresser. Every branch in Me that does not bear fruit, He takes away; and every branch that bears fruit, He prunes it, that it may bear more fruit." John 15:1-2

God the Father planted the True Vine in this world for a specific purpose; *"For God did not send the Son into the world to judge the world, but that the world should be saved through Him," John 3:17.* This old lost and sinful world which included you and I was destined to suffer the wages of our sin which is death, eternal separation from God in hell. Jesus said, *"For the Son of Man has come to seek and save that which was lost," Luke 19:10.* He went to the cross to accomplish our redemption from sin and death. Since then many lost souls have by faith attached themselves to the True Vine and received His salvation. *"For the grace of God has appeared, bringing salvation to all men, instructing us to deny ungodliness and worldly desires and to live sensibly, righteously, and godly in the present age, looking for the blessed hope and the appearing of the glory of our great God and Savior, Christ Jesus; who gave Himself for us, that He might redeem us from every lawless deed and purify for Himself a people for His own possession, zealous for good deeds." Titus 2:11-14.*

Jesus is perfectly sinless and holy and therefore requires a bride who is sinless and holy. He knows that we are all unclean and completely incapable of making ourselves holy and blameless apart from Him. So Jesus our bridegroom provided what was necessary to accomplish our cleansing and sanctification.

"Husbands, love your wives, just as Christ also loved the church and gave Himself up for her; that He might sanctify her, and cleanse her by the washing of water with the word, that He might present her to Himself the church in all her glory, having no spot or wrinkle or any such thing; but that she should be holy and blameless." Ephesians 5:25-27. Since providing a holy and blameless bride for His Son is God the Father's purpose for redeeming us, He the Devine Vinedresser has to take away the fruitless branches and prune the fruitful branches. This pruning in our lives though painful is necessary for our sanctification and our fruitfulness. For without it we would remain sinful wretches unworthy to serve as the bride of Messiah. Notice that the Devine Vinedresser accomplishes the pruning that we can never do ourselves. Only His skill and knowledge can determine what really needs to be pruned from our lives. The branches have no say in the matter, they only submit to His skillful hand. *All discipline for the moment seems not to be joyful, but sorrowful; yet to those who have been trained by it, afterwards it yields the peaceful fruit of righteousness. For those whom the LORD loves He disciplines, and He scourges every son whom He receives." Hebrews 12:11, 6.*

Now this does not imply that the loss of a loved one is God's discipline in our lives or that God is punishing us for some sin. But God does allow such trials in our lives to sanctify us and create in us a purer, undistracted love for Him. Job who after losing all his children proclaimed, *"Naked I came from my mother's womb, and naked I shall return there. The LORD gave and the Lord has taken away. Blessed be the name of the LORD." Job 1:21.*

Prayer: Heavenly Father, Thank you for your perfect pruning that we can become a pure and chaste bride fit for your holy Son. Lord I submit to the hand who holds the shears so that I might be purified, bear much fruit for you, and bring glory to your name which you have given to us as the bride of Messiah. In His precious name I pray, Amen.

"Abide in Me, and I in you. As the branch cannot bear fruit of itself, unless it abides in the vine, so neither can you, unless you abide in Me. I am the vine, you are the branches; he who abides in Me, and I in him, he bears much fruit; for apart from Me you can do nothing." John 15:4-5

One day I decided to have a bagel for breakfast. So I got my bagel, sliced it, put it in the toaster, and pushed the toast button down. Then I waited; and waited; and waited for my bagel to pop up. But it never did because I discovered that the toaster was unplugged. My bagel did not toast because the toaster had no power to do the job it was designed to do. It was useless because it was disconnected from the power source. The same thing is true of us if we as branches are not abiding in the True Vine. We are called to be His witnesses, His servants, His ambassadors, His prayer warriors and so on, but unless we are vitally connected to Jesus we are as useless as an unplugged toaster. Jesus promised His disciples; *"But you shall receive power when the Holy Spirit has come upon you,"* Acts 1:8. Unfortunately, much of today's ministry done by Jesus' disciples is fruitless because it is done apart from Him and His power. Only God can forgive sins, save lost souls, heal the brokenhearted, resurrect the dead, and take people to heaven. There is nothing that we can do to improve a lost soul's condition apart from Jesus. Only He can save from sin and death. *"What man can live and not see death?" Psalm 89:48.* The mortality rate for all created human beings is 100% so far. Jesus' disciples asked; *"Then who can be saved?" And looking upon them Jesus said to them, "With men this is impossible, but with God all things are possible," Matthew 19:25-26.*

After witnessing the death of a loved one we become more painfully aware of how frail, how powerless, and how helpless we human's are. If I could have done anything to keep my beloved Linda here, I would have. But I was completely helpless and powerless to do anything. I had no choice but to surrender her into the loving arms of Jesus. He is Linda's Lord and God, Savior and Messiah, and her eternal well-being is His duty. He had bought her with His own blood and she is now His to have and to hold for all eternity. My duty to have and to hold until death do us part was completed and she now holds His nailed scarred hand.

Jesus, however, has not left me here alone. I am here to serve Him, to accomplish His purpose for my life, to bear much fruit and bring Him glory. Fortunately I not only abide in Jesus, He also abides in me. I can love the brethren, have compassion on the lost, and bring them all to the Savior only because Jesus abides in me. *"I have been crucified with Christ; it is no longer I who live, but Christ lives in me; and the life which I now live in the flesh I live by faith in the Son of God, who loved me, and delivered Himself up for me." Galatians 2:20.*

Prayer: Beloved Vine; Thank You for the precious proposal to abide in You. Thank You Jesus for the precious promise, that as we abide in You that You are faithful to abide in us. Praise You, Lord that in You we have the power to bear fruit and that it is only because You, Precious Bridegroom abide in us. Thank You, Jesus, that in You I can fulfill Your purpose for this branch and bear Your fruit. Hold me fast dear Vine, Amen.

"If you abide in Me, and My words abide in you, ask whatever you wish, and it shall be done for you. By this is My Father glorified, that you bear much fruit, and so prove to be My disciples." John 15:7-8

When I think about what it means to abide with Jesus my mind focuses on the person who spent the most time with Him while He was here on earth. That person is His mother Mary, who had known Him from His Holy Spirit conception until His crucifixion on Calvary. Mary witnessed His first wobbly steps, heard His first stammering words, and listen everyday as Jesus shared what He learned in Hebrew school. Mary treasured all the memories of His early childhood and watched as *"And Jesus kept increasing in wisdom and stature, and in favor with God and men," Luke 2:52.* Sometime after Jesus had grown up to become a young man Mary most likely became a widow, because there is no mention of Joseph in the bible after Jesus was twelve years old. This meant that as the first-born son, Jesus took on the responsibility of head the household. Mary learned to trust Jesus to provide for every need of their growing family. Mary must have known what Jesus meant when He said, *"Ask whatever you wish, and it shall be done for you," John 15:7.*

One day the family of Jesus was invited to a friend's wedding. When the host ran out of wine Mary naturally went to her provider Jesus and simply said, *"They have no wine."* Jesus responded by turning 150 gallons of water into wine that was better than that which the headwaiter had previously served. This was a miraculous answer to Mary's prayer. *"This beginning of His signs Jesus did in Cana of Galilee, and manifested His glory, and His disciples believed in Him," John 2:11.*

Dear brothers and sisters in Jesus. We are blessed to be a part of one great big family where Jesus, God's First-born, is head. *And stretching out His hand toward His disciples, He said, "Behold, My mother and My brothers! For whoever does the will of My Father who is in heaven, he is My brother and sister and mother," Matthew 12:49-50.* This is not an exclusive group reserved only for the worthy, the invitation is offered to all who wish to believe and receive God's First-born Son, Jesus. *"But as many as received Him, to them He gave the right to become children of God, even to those who believe in His name, who were born not of blood, nor of the will of the flesh, nor of the will of man, but of God,"*

John 1:12-13. What a blessing to be children of God who can always come to Jesus with our every prayer requests and have them answered according to His will. "Tis so sweet to trust in Jesus, Just to take Him at His word, Just to rest upon His promise, Just to know "Thus saith the Lord," Louisa M R Stead. Jesus wants us to bear much fruit, glorify His Father and prove to be His disciples and is more than willing to provide whatever we need to accomplish these goals. When our children do well we say, "That's my boy", or "That's my girl". They bring joy to our hearts at such moments.

"Now to Him who is able to do exceeding abundantly beyond all that we ask or think, according to the power that works within us, to Him be the glory in the church and in Christ Jesus to all generations forever and ever. Amen", Ephesians 3:20-21.

Prayer: Thank you Jesus for your promise to answer our prayers. Thank you that as members of your family that we can trust You to provide everything we need to bring glory to our heavenly Father and honor to your name as your disciples. Thank You Jesus that You are He who gives to His beloved even in his sleep. May we bear much fruit and enlarge your Kingdom. Amen.

Jesus Loves You As the Father Loved Him John 15:9-10

"Just as the Father loved Me, I have also loved you; abide in My love. If you keep My commandments, you will abide in My love; just as I have kept My Father's commandments, and abide in His love." John15:9-10

Before starting His public ministry Jesus went down to the Jordan River to be baptized by John the Baptist. When Jesus arose from the water *"the Holy Spirit descended upon Him in bodily form like a dove, and a voice came out of heaven, "Thou art My beloved Son, in Thee I am well- pleased," Luke 3:22.* What blessed words for any son to hear from his father. I love you and am well pleased with what you are doing. It is hard for us finite human beings to fathom the love of an infinite eternal God for His only begotten Son. It is a love that has no beginning and no end, a love with no limits, no ulterior motives, a love that is holy and awesome, and a love that never fails. The closest description that I can find is the Apostle Paul's love discourse in 1 Corinthians 13:4-8. *Love is patient, love is kind, and is not jealous; love does not brag and is not arrogant, does not act unbecomingly; it does not seek its own, is not provoked, does not take into account a wrong suffered, does not rejoice in unrighteousness, but rejoices with the truth; bears all things, believes all things, hopes all things, endures all things. Love never fails.* But God's love is better demonstrated than defined. *We know love by this, that He laid down His life for us; and we ought to lay down our lives for the brethren, 1 John 3:16.* God could have given up on His prize creation, mankind. He could have said I have had enough with these hardhearted ungrateful creatures. God could have left us to suffer forever in hell for our sins, but His Father's heart just would not let Him and He sent the Son of His love on a rescue mission. Jesus showed us the love of His Father by His obedience. *And being found in appearance as a man, He humbled Himself by becoming obedient to the point of death, even death on a cross. Therefore also God highly exalted Him, and bestowed on Him the name which is above every name, Philippians 2:8-9.*

What a blessed place to abide, in the love of Jesus, which is the love of His Father. Young children love to imitate their parents. They want to be like daddy or mommy. We as God's little ones should have a heart to be like our heavenly Father and live our lives to please Him. If we do we will abide in His Love. In 1981 when I was baptized the event was attended by my parents and grandparents who had prayed long and hard for my salvation. They loved me and were quite pleased with me on that day. After I came up out of the water the congregation sang the old children's hymn, Jesus Loves Me, because my testimony was about how much Jesus had loved me. And since then I continue to learn daily how much He loves me as I abide in His Love. What a blessed place to dwell, what peace, what comfort, and what joy are found in the love of Jesus and God our Father. *He who dwells in the shelter of the Most High will abide in the shadow of the Almighty. For you have made the LORD, my refuge, even the Most High, your dwelling place. No evil will befall you, nor will any plague come near your tent; For He will give His angels charge concerning you, to guard you in all your ways. Because he has loved Me, therefore I will deliver him; I will set him securely on high, because he has known My name. He will call upon Me, and I will answer him; I will be with him in trouble; I will rescue him, and honor him. With a long life I will satisfy him, and let him behold My salvation, Psalm 91:1, 9-11, 14-16.*

Prayer: Thank you Jesus for abiding in your Father's love and being obedient to Him unto death on a cross. Thank you for the promise of your love to those who trust and obey you. Thank you that you did not wait for us to come to you, but you came from heaven for us. Amen.

"These things I have spoken to you, that My joy may be in you, and that your joy may be made full," John 15:11

You know it's easy to be joyful when the circumstances in your life are going well. It's natural to sing, smile and praise the Lord when things are going our way. But how can we rejoice when the bottom collapses and all hell seems to break loose in our lives? How can we have joy when our hearts are breaking over the loss of a loved one?

The Bible says, *Rejoice in the Lord always; again I will say, rejoice! Philippians 4:4.* But how is that possible? The servant of Jesus who wrote those words was suffering in a Roman prison at the time. On another occasion he and a partner were beaten with rods and thrown into a prison at Philippi for casting an evil spirit out of a girl. We read how they responded in Acts 16:25, *But about midnight Paul and Silas were praying and singing hymns of praise to God, and the prisoners were listening to them.* Even though they had been beaten and thrown into prison for serving the Lord, Paul and Silas had joy in their hearts. Where did this joy come from? I assure that their joy was not in their circumstances. We are not told to rejoice in our circumstances always. Their joy was in the Lord and we are commanded to rejoice in the Lord.

Where did Paul and Silas get this Joy? What is the source of their bliss? Paul lists joy as the second of the nine fruits of the Holy Spirit in Galatians 5:22. Jesus was referring to the Holy Spirit when He said, *"He who believes in Me, as the Scripture said, From his inner-most being shall flow rivers of living water,"* John 7:38. Every person who puts their faith in Jesus for their salvation is baptized by Jesus with the Holy Spirit. Every follower of Jesus has this source of joy dwelling inside them. That's why many of them could face being burned alive or devoured by wild beasts, with joyful praising of the Lord that they would not deny. They knew what it was like to, *"Consider it all joy, my brethren, when you encounter various trials,"* James 1:2

In Hebrews we are encouraged to, *"run with endurance the race set before us, fixing our eyes on Jesus, the author and perfecter of faith, who for the joy set before Him endured the cross, despising the shame, and has sat down at the right hand of the throne of God,"* Hebrews 12:1-2. If our Lord Jesus can joyfully endure the cross for us, what can we not endure for Him. We know that Jesus sat down at the right hand of the throne of God after His suffering and He has promised a home in glory for His faithful ones who may be called upon to endure sorrow for a brief time on this earth. Hold on dear hurting soul, *"Weeping may last for the night, but a shout of joy comes in the morning,"* Psalm 30:5. The prophet Isaiah sings, *"Behold, God is my salvation, I will trust and not be afraid; For the LORD God is my strength and song, and He has become my salvation. Therefore you will joyously draw water from the springs of salvation,"* Isaiah 12:2-3.

Prayer: Thank you Jesus for the joy you give us in midst of our sorrows. And thank you dear Savior for the river of living water that you have placed in our inner-most being. Help us Lord to keep our eyes fixed on you as we finish the race that you call us to run for your glory. Amen.

Jesus Commands Us to Love One Another John 15:12

"This is My commandment, that you love one another, just as I have loved you," John 15:12

To Jesus love is a verb, an action word. When you look at His ministry life in the four Gospels, Jesus was the Energizer Bunny of love. He was constantly reaching out to people, healing their sicknesses, casting out their demons, forgiving their sins, calming their storms, feeding their hunger, teaching them to pray and seek after His Father plus many other things. John concludes his Gospel with these words, *"And there are also many other things which Jesus did, which if they were written in detail, I suppose that even the world itself would not contain the books which were written,"* John 21:25.

Jesus not only commanded His disciples to love another, He taught by example. John uses His greatest example to teach us how to roll up our sleeves and put ourselves out for others. *"We know love by this that He laid down His life for us; and we ought to lay down our lives for the brethren. But whoever has this world's goods, and beholds his brother in need and closes his heart against him, how does the love of God abide in him? Little children, let us not love with word or with tongue, but in deed and truth,"* 1 John 3:16-18.

I have been a needy brother many times in my life and witnessed the love of Jesus poured out to me and my family many times. Brothers and sisters gave their money, cars, housing, helped me find jobs, cleaned our home, provided meals, and performed many acts of love when we were in need. I have witnessed the body of Christ in action and it is a most beautiful thing.

One person who stands out as a great lover for Jesus is a woman named Margaret, a lonely widow. When my grandmother grew gravely sick and was unable to take care of her home, her family and herself Margaret was there every day meeting her needs. This was before the time of paid nurses or companions coming into homes to care for the hurting. None of those services were available to the common people of Northeast Philadelphia back then. But they had Margaret, who not only helped my grandmother in her time of need; she cared for my aunt and many other infirmed and widowed women simply out of love for Jesus. When my grandmother passed, my grandfather made one of the wisest decisions of his life by asking Margaret to become his second wife. When I was a wee lad I used to tag along with Grammy Margaret as she made her rounds visiting shut-in widowed women to take care of their needs. She would give them rides to church to worship Jesus and when they were unable to make it to church she would take Jesus to them. Grammy Margaret was a great example of the love of Jesus in action for most of her adult life.

"Beloved, if God so loved us, we also ought to love one another. No one has beheld God at any time; if we love one another, God abides in us, and His love is perfected in us," 1 John 4:11-12.

Prayer: Dear Jesus, It seems like an awesome challenge for us to love one another as You have loved us. Especially in light of the way You have loved us. Lord help us to be faithful to You in our love for one another. And thank You for showing us other brothers and sisters who have shared your love with us. May You be glorified and the lost won by Your love in us. Amen.

"Greater love has no one than this, that one lay down his life for his friends. You are My friends, if you do what I command you," John 15:13-14

They call it the ultimate sacrifice, one giving his life so that others might live. You may have heard about the young Marine who dove on a grenade to save his squad. Or the New York firefighters who rushed into the burning World Trade Center buildings to rescue those trapped inside and never appeared again. History holds many such selfless acts of bravery and self-sacrifice. All the men who had heard these words of Jesus gave their lives for Him and His Gospel. And since then many disciples of Jesus have followed them and have given their lives for the sake of His mission. They indeed were, *"men of whom the world was not worthy."*

One of the most difficult griefs we can suffer is the loss of a young person, seemingly cut off before his prime. Many parents have seen young children die of sudden illness or injury. Some have prayed earnestly and witnessed loved ones miraculously saved from sure death, while many more others have prayed no less earnestly only to watch their beloved little ones perish. In the Bible King David was one who prayed and fasted for the life of his little child. This is what he said after the child died, *"While the child was still alive, I fasted and wept; for I said, 'Who knows, the LORD may be gracious to me, that the child may live.' But now he has died; why should I fast? Can I bring him back again? I shall go to him, but he will not return to me," 2 Samuel 12:22-23.* David was comforted by the hope that his child was in Heaven with the LORD and that he would someday go to him. Parents who know Jesus have this hope also, that they will see their child again, to comfort them.

One testimony that I heard was one of a father whose son was dying of cancer. He said to his son, I wish I could take the cancer from your body, place that cancer in my body, and die in your place. Most loving parents would understand his wish and would desire to do the same for their child if they were faced with the same circumstances. God looked down from Heaven and saw us helpless sinners facing the wages of our sin. He knew that unless He intervened we would all be eternally lost in hell. *"But God demonstrates His own love toward us, in that while we were yet sinners, Christ died for us," Romans 5:8.* Jesus made the ultimate sacrifice for us on the cross to take away the curse of our sin, which is death, and open up the gates of Heaven for us. Isaiah says, *"Surely our griefs He Himself bore, and our sorrows He carried; yet we ourselves esteemed Him stricken, smitten by God, and afflicted. But He was pierced through for our transgressions, He was crushed for our iniquities; the chastening for our well-being fell upon Him, and by His scourging we are healed. All of us like sheep have gone astray, each of us has turned to his own way; But the LORD has caused the iniquity of us all to fall on Him,"*
Isaiah 53:4-6.

Prayer: Dear Jesus, Thank You for giving the greatest love on the cross of Calvary for us. And thank You for your servants who gave their lives for the sake of the Gospel. Worthy is the Lamb who was slain to receive all glory, honor and power. May we be faithful unto death until death is no more and we live together with You, Jesus. Thank You for your example of love. Amen.

"No longer do I call you slaves, for the slave does not know what his master is doing; but I have called you friends, for all things that I have heard from My Father I have made known to you," John 15:15

"But I have called you friends", says the Son of God, the King of kings and the Lord of lords. A God who calls His followers friends is unheard of in this world. What god in history has ever called his followers friends? Every other religion created by man is a works religion, meaning that the followers had to do something in order to appease their god. A system of laws is always employed that requires strict obedience. Even Jehovah of the Old Testament commanded obedience from His people and only a few were called His friends. In fact only Moses was permitted to enter the tent of meeting to speak with God. Everyone else had to remain outside. *"Thus the LORD used to speak to Moses face to face, just as a man speaks to his friend," Exodus 33:11.* A system of sacrifices was commanded in order for sinful men to make atonement. Access to God was not possible until man's sin could be removed.

God in His love could not stand to remain separated from His most precious creation, us. *"But when the fulness of the time came, God sent forth His Son, born of a woman, born under the Law, in order that He might redeem those who were under the Law, that we might receive the adoption as sons," Galatians 4:4-5.* On the eve of His sacrifice on a Roman cross Jesus establishes a new relationship with His disciples. He said, *"No longer do I call you slaves; ..... but I have called you friends."* Jesus came to provide a perfect once for all atoning sacrifice for our sins so that we can now have unhindered access to God. *"But He (Jesus), having offered one sacrifice for sins for all time, sat down at the right hand of God. For by one offering He has perfected for all time those who are sanctified. And the Holy Spirit also bears witness to us; for after saying, 'This is the covenant that I will make with them, after those days, says the LORD; I will put My Laws upon their heart, and upon their mind I will write them.' He then says, 'And their sins and their lawless deeds I will remember no more.' Since therefore, brethren, we have confidence to enter the holy place by the blood of Jesus, by a new and living way which He inaugurated for us through the veil, that is, His flesh, let us draw near with a sincere heart in full assurance of faith, having our hearts sprinkled clean from an evil conscience and our bodies washed with pure water," Hebrews 10:12, 14-17, 19, 22.*

Jesus now resides in Heaven where He intercedes for us with the Father. His throne room is always open to us 24 hours a day, 7 days a week. We are invited to come before Jesus to speak with Him face to face as Moses did in the tent of meeting. Whatever our concerns or whatever our circumstances we have a faithful compassionate friend in Jesus. We have been set free from our slavery to sin, and works of law. Free to talk with Jesus. *Jesus stood and cried out, saying, "If any man is thirsty, let him come to Me and drink," John 7:37.*

Prayer: Dear Jesus, Thank You for making us Your friends, who can come into Your presence at any time. Thank You that You made the way and we do not have to do anything to merit an audience with our King. May our times of communion with You be sweet and refreshing. Amen.

"You did not choose Me, but I chose you, and appointed you, that you should go and bear fruit, and that your fruit should remain, that whatever you ask of the Father in My name, He may give to you," John 15:16

Both my wife and daughter were adopted as children. Which means that the parents who conceived them could not keep them for some reason and new parents had to be found to provide a home for them and raise them. Adoptive parents hire a lawyer, spend a lot of money, and pass stringent evaluations before they can adopt a child. They are then presented with children that they can choose to adopt. These become special chosen children who receive the same rights and same love as any child born naturally to parents. Before they were adopted they were orphans with no permanent homes or families to care for them. They were alone without hope is this unforgiving world. But God in His mercy provided homes for them where they can be valued, loved, protected and provided for. It is not a shameful thing to be adopted, but a blessed privilege given by God. Adopted children are not second class children, they are as valued and wanted as much as naturally born children. They can better understand the grace of God and His adoption of lost souls because they were saved from a life of hopelessness, stress and poverty.

Our loving Heavenly Father saw that we were also lost and without hope in this unforgiving world. *"Remember that you were at that time separate from Christ, excluded from the commonwealth of Israel, and strangers to the covenants of promise, having no hope and without God in the world. But now in Christ Jesus you who were far off have been brought near by the blood of Christ," Ephesians 2:12-13.* Sometimes when we lose loved ones we feel like orphans, left behind with no one to love us. That is when we should remember the Father who loves us more than anyone else can. We are all children of God, with a Father who loves us, a multitude of brothers and sisters, an eternal home, and a secure inheritance. God paid the highest price for our adoption. *"You were not redeemed with perishable things like silver or gold from your futile way of life inherited from your forefathers, but with precious blood, as of a lamb unblemished and spotless, the blood of Christ," 1 Peter 1:18-19.* How much are you valued by your Heavenly Father? He sacrificed His most precious Son to adopt you. We are not abandoned to face this cold world alone. We are part of a forever family. *"But when the fulness of the time came, God sent forth His Son, born of a woman, born under the Law, in order that He might redeem those who were under the Law, that we might receive the adoption as sons. And because you are sons, God has sent forth the Spirit of His Son into our hearts, crying, Abba! Father! Therefore you are no longer a slave, but a son; and if a son, then an heir through God," Galatians 4:4-7*

Prayer: Dear Heavenly Father, Thank You for giving your only Son, Jesus, to adopt us as Your own children. Thank You for Your constant love and care. Thank You for holding us when we hurt and restoring us in Your love to become children that bear fruit and bring glory to Your name. In Jesus precious name we pray. Amen.

"This I command you, that you love one another," John 15:17

When God says something three times it must be very important to Him. In John 13:34, John 15:12, and John 15:17 Jesus commands His disciples to *"love one another."* It is to be love that marks us as His disciples. In fact John in His First Epistle states that if we do not have love for one another, then we are really not true believers walking in the manner of Jesus. *"The one who says he is in the light and yet hates his brother is in the darkness until now. The one who loves his brother abides in the light and there is no cause for stumbling in him,"* 1 John 2:9-10. Love assures us that we are His. *"We know that we have passed out of death into life, because we love the brethren. He who does not love abides in death. We shall know by this that we are of the truth, and shall assure our heart before Him,"* 1 John 3:14, 19.

When my wife, Linda, suddenly left me for Heaven one of the greatest things that helped me endure that horrible tragedy is the outpouring of love from my brothers and sisters in Jesus. I have been blessed to have true believers alive both in my family and in my church. There were several of them in my home within minutes of my calling for help. I received comfort, prayers, financial help, meals and many things that I have since forgotten about. Friends were there to help plan the celebration of Linda's ascension with wonderful worship music and great encouragement. This love did not start when my wife passed on. It was there 25 years before when as a hurting young believer I first walked into that church. I was greeted so warmly with genuine love for Jesus that I decided to make the church my home. It was there that I learned to love like Jesus reaching out with compassion to those in need both within the church and outside of it.

"Beloved, let us love one another, for love is from God; and everyone who loves is born of God and knows God. The one who does not love does not know God, for God is love. By this the love of God was manifested in us, that God has sent His only begotten Son into the world so that we might live through Him. In this is love, not that we loved God, but that He loved us and sent His Son to be the propitiation for our sins. Beloved, if God so loved us, we also ought to love one another. No one has beheld God at any time; if we love one another, God abides in us, and His love is perfected in us," 1 John 4:7-12.

The blessing is that God Himself abides in the hearts of His loving children producing even more love to His glory. Love is a generous giving thing. God gave His Son. Jesus laid down His life. The body of Jesus His church continues that outpouring of love as He abides in us. Lost and hurting souls meet the Savior through the love of those who are truly His. *"Let us hold fast the confession of our hope without wavering, for He who promised is faithful; and let us consider how to stimulate one another to love and good deeds,"* Hebrews 10: 23-24.

Prayer: Thank You Lord God for giving us Your Son. And thank You Jesus that Your love was poured out for us through Your body on the cross of Calvary. Lord our hearts are assured of Your presence when Your love is poured out through us. Lord Jesus be glorified even more as You pour out Your love through Your body, the church. Amen.

"If the world hates you, you know that it has hated Me before it hated you. If you were of the world, the world would love its own; but because you are not of the world, but I have chose you out of the world, therefore the world hates you," John 15:18-19

It started early in Jesus' life. As a tiny boy Herod the Great tried to murder little Jesus. He killed several other baby boys in Bethlehem but God warned Joseph to flee to Egypt thereby sparing God's Son. Later, at the end of Jesus' earthly life, before the Roman Governor Pilate the angry mob cried out, "Crucify Him! Crucify Him!" Even though Pilate found no guilt in Jesus demanding death, he gave into their demands and sent Him away to be crucified and had a murderer, Barabbas released instead. The reason stated was that Jesus claimed to be God. Men have never been neutral toward God. Either they embraced Him or they rebelled against Him killing the messengers that He sent and choosing false gods.

Jesus called His disciples to take His message of salvation to a world that despises Him. Many have chosen to, like Jesus, become obedient unto death. The hallowed list of martyrs is long, some are well known, others are known by only a few, but all are known by the King for which they laid down their lives. Each has left loved ones behind in a hostile world. The list unfortunately continues to grow as followers of Jesus are targeted by those who hate Him today. Thank God there are organizations that are able to reach out with compassion to some of those who are left grieving the loss of these precious saints. Many are given the basic necessities of life denied to them by their persecutors. Others are given the resources and strength to go on in faith and rebuild their lives in the aftermath of incredible tragedy. In such places the church grows as result of their sacrifices. They can dispose of His disciples but the body of Jesus keeps growing.

Two such places were found among the seven churches that Jesus addresses in Revelation chapter two. *"And to the angel of the church of Smyrna write: The first and the last, who was dead, and has come to life, says this: 'I know your tribulation and your poverty (but you are rich), and the blasphemy by those who say they are Jews and are not, but are a synagogue of Satan. Do not fear what you are about to suffer. Behold, the devil is about to cast some of you into prison, that you may be tested, and you will have tribulation ten days. Be faithful until death, and I will give you the crown of life'. And to the angel of the church in Pergamum write: The One who has the sharp two-edged sword says this: 'I know where you dwell, where Satan's throne is; and you hold fast My name, and did not deny My faith, even in the days of Antipas, My witness, My faithful one, who was killed among you, where Satan dwells. He who has an ear, let him hear what the Spirit says to the churches. To him who overcomes, to him I will give some of the hidden manna, and I will give him a white stone, and a new name written on the stone which no one knows but he who receives it.'"Revelation 2:8-10, 12-13, 17.*

Prayer: Dear Lord Jesus, We praise You that You have endured great suffering and death on a cross for us. Thank You for Your servants who were willing to give their lives for the sake of Your gospel so that today we may know You. In Jesus name we pray, Amen.

"Remember the word that I said to you, 'A slave is not greater than his master.' If they persecuted Me, they will also persecute you; if they kept my word, they will keep yours also. But all these things they will do to you for My name's sake, because they do not know the One who sent Me," John 15:20-21.

One of the first books that I read as a young Christian was, Vanya by Myrna Grant. It is the true story of a Russian youth, Ivan Moisiev, who was drafted into the Soviet Red Army at the age of seventeen. While serving his country this young believer was tortured and murdered by his comrades in the communist military for his faith in Jesus. The book includes photographs of his tortured body taken by his family before his burial. Even though I never met this young man or his family, the testimony recorded in this book of his life and courageous faith kindled in me and other readers a greater love for Jesus and stronger faith in Him.

Why talk about such horrible things? How can such stories of terrible suffering comfort anyone who is grieving the loss of a loved one? Well two reasons come to mind. First such stories are glorious testimonies of faith, love and courage in the face of suffering and death. Second witnessing the suffering of other believers helps us get a sense that we are not alone in our suffering. That there are many others who have felt deep sorrow and even suffered more than we have. Suffering has been the lot of the faithful since Adam and Eve witnessed their first born son, Cain; slay his brother Abel in Genesis chapter four. The story of God's people has been a tragic one ever since. The New Testament brings more tragic stories of a Savior who died on a cross and His followers being stoned to death and beheaded because of opposition to the message of the gospel of Jesus. The Apostle Paul warns young Timothy, *"And indeed all who desire to live godly in Christ Jesus will be persecuted," 2 Timothy 3:12.*

So then why follow Jesus? Couldn't we avoid all this suffering by not making any waves about our faith and upsetting the unbelievers? Perhaps, if all we had to be concerned about is the here and now. But there is an eternity and those who do not know Jesus face a suffering in hell that will never end and will be more intense than anything we will experience on this earth. Love compels us and God commands us to go and make disciples.

Besides all that Jesus gives a blessing to those who suffer injustice for Him. *"Blessed are those who have been persecuted for the sake of righteousness, for theirs is the kingdom of heaven. Blessed are you when men cast insults at you, and persecute you, and say all kinds of evil against you falsely, on account of Me. Rejoice, and be glad, for your reward in heaven is great, for so they persecuted the prophets who were before you," Matthew 5:10-12.*

Prayer: Dear Lord Jesus, Thank You for the testimony of Vanya who loved You unto death. May his love for You inspire us to a greater love for You. Lord, help us to see Your purpose for all that has happened and for why we are here. Comfort us as we mourn our losses and even suffer for You. Give us the courage and strength to be faithful until we see You coming in the clouds. For Your glory we pray, Amen.

"If I had not come and spoken to them, they would not have sin, but now they have no excuse for their sin. He who hates Me hates My Father also. If I had not done the works which no one else did, they would not have sin; but now they have both seen and hated Me and My Father as well. But they have done this in order that the word may be fulfilled that is written in their law, 'They hated Me without a cause.' " John 15:22-25.

When Adam disobeyed God and ate of the fruit that God said not to eat he tried to excuse his sin saying, *"The woman whom Thou gavest to be with me, she gave me from the tree, and I ate,"* *Genesis 3:12.* Adam tried to point the finger at Eve but God was not buying it, and brought severe punishment on him for his sin. Adam enjoyed perfect fellowship with God in Eden until he ate the fruit, was banished from the garden and brought death to himself and all of his descendants. The consequences of sin are grave. The Apostle Paul tells us that the wages of sin is death.

Jesus came and preached eternal life to all those who would believe in Him. Jesus demonstrated His divine authority to give eternal life by performing miraculous works that only God could do. The purpose for all His miracles is stated in

John 20:30-31; *"Many other signs therefore Jesus also performed in the presence of the disciples, which are not written in this book; but these have been written that you may believe that Jesus is the Christ, the Son of God; and that believing you may have life in His name."* The ultimate sin *committed* by those who hated Jesus was to reject Him and His offer of eternal life. Only those who hate God will suffer eternity separated from Him. *But Jesus said, "I came that they might have life, and might have it abundantly. I am the good shepherd; the good shepherd lays down His life for the sheep."* John 10:10-11. The people who heard Jesus speak and witnessed His miracles had a choice to believe Jesus was God's Messiah or reject Him. We all have the same choice love Jesus and receive eternal life, or hate Jesus and receive the wages of your sin.

I know my wife Linda loved Jesus and put her faith in Him as her Savior and as a result she now abides with Jesus in Heaven. This is the hope we have for all those who love Jesus that when their days on this earth come to end that they shall ascend to be with their Savior in Heaven. Paul tells us; *"Therefore, being always of good courage, and knowing that while we are at home in the body we are absent from the Lord - for we walk by faith, not by sight — we are of good courage, I say, and prefer rather to be absent from the body and to be at home with the Lord."* 2 Corinthians 5:6-8. What a wonderful promise we have in Jesus and what a comfort we have in knowing that our loved ones who loved Jesus go to live with Him when they pass away. Peter said, *"And there is salvation in no one else; for there is no other name given under heaven that has been given among men, by which we must be saved."* Acts 4:12. We, like all other descendants of Adam, deserve to die for our sins, but God in His mercy sent His Son Jesus to die on the cross in our place so that we may have eternal life in Jesus.

Prayer: Jesus thank you for Your words and Your works whereby we can believe in You as our Messiah. Thank You for the promise that those who love and trust in You will abide with You in Heaven when our time on earth is done. Lord help us share this message of hope with those who do not yet know You and believe in You. Amen.

"When the Helper comes, whom I will send to you from the Father, that is the Spirit of truth who proceeds from the Father, He will bear witness of Me, and you will bear witness also, because you have been with Me from the beginning." John 15: 26-27.

Jesus promised His disciples a Helper who will help them with what they must do after He ascends to Heaven. He is the Spirit of truth who will bear witness of Him.

What is the Spirit's testimony? *"And it is the Spirit who bears witness, because the Spirit is the truth. The one who believes in the Son of God has the witness in himself; the one who does not believe God has made Him a liar, because he has not believed in the witness that God has borne concerning His Son. And the witness is this, that God has given us eternal life, and this life is in His Son. He who has the Son has the life; he who does not have the Son of God does not have the life." 1 John 5:7, 10-12.* Eternal life is for everyone who believes in Jesus. When did we receive this eternal life? We received it when we first put our faith in Jesus. How long will eternal life last? Forever we will be with the Lord. Do you have the Son? Then you have eternal life.

"For all who are being led by the Spirit of God, these are sons of God. For you have not received a spirit of slavery leading to fear again, but you have received a spirit of adoption as sons by which we cry out, 'Abba! Father!' The Spirit Himself bears witness with our spirit that we are children of God, and if children, heirs also, heirs of God and fellow heirs with Christ, if indeed we suffer with Him in order that we may also be glorified with Him." Romans 8:14-17. What a blessing to know that we are children of God, and fellow heirs with Christ! This is the Helper's witness. We have a home in Heaven. *"For I consider that the sufferings of this present time are not worthy to be compared with the glory that is to be revealed to us." Romans 8:18.* Our loved ones who have passed into Heaven have already seen the glory of God, which they will someday share with us when we join them. My mother-in-law used to say whenever we were suffering through hard times, "This too shall pass". Fortunately our times of sorrow will be short lived. Joy is coming in the mourning. It will be an eternal joy with the Giver of all joy forever.

"Blessed be the God and Father of our Lord Jesus Christ, who according to His great mercy has caused us to be born again to a living hope through the resurrection of Jesus Christ from the dead, to obtain an inheritance which is imperishable and undefiled and will not fade away, reserved in Heaven for you, who are protected by the power of God through faith for a salvation ready to be revealed in the last time." 1 Peter 1:3-5.

Prayer: Thank you Father for sending us Your Helper to witness to us the blessing that You have prepared for us in Your Son Jesus Christ. Lord Helper helps us through these times of sorrow to the inheritance we will share in Christ. Father, may the knowledge that You have adopted us as Your own children bring us much comfort. We look forward to the time when we all will be home with You forever! Thank You Jesus for making it all possible by Your sacrifice on the cross. We will be eternally grateful. Amen.

"These things I have spoken to you, that you may be kept from stumbling." John 16:1.

When we are going through times of grief we are most vulnerable to stumble and do things that are not pleasing to God. We can be tempted to comfort ourselves in self-destructive ways. Jesus wants us to continue to stand against the schemes of the devil. *"Finally, be strong in the Lord, and in the strength of His might. Put on the full armor of God, that you may be able to stand firm against the schemes of the devil." Ephesians 6:10-11.*

Has God given us any help against temptation? Yes, He does not only help, God provides a way of escape. *"Therefore let him who thinks he stands take heed lest he fall. No temptation has overtaken you but such is common to man; and God is faithful, who will not allow you to be tempted beyond what you are able, but with the temptation will provide the way of escape also, that you may be able to endure it." 1 Corinthians 10:12-13.* When being tempted look for God's way of escape.

When Jesus taught His disciples to pray He gave them these words: *"Our Father who art in heaven, Hallowed be thy name. Thy kingdom come, Thy will be done, On earth as it is in heaven. Give us this day our daily bread. And forgive us our debts, as we also have forgiven our debtors. And do not lead us into temptation, but deliver us from evil." Matthew 6:9-13.* If we allow ourselves to be led by our Father in heaven, we will avoid temptation and be delivered from evil.

David King of Israel was called a man after God's heart because he had a close relationship with the Lord. He went through many trials in his life and offers this testimony as how God blessed him: *"Bless our God, O peoples, and sound His praise abroad. Who keeps us in life, and does not allow our feet to slip. For Thou hast tried us, O God; Thou hast refined us as silver is refined. Thou didst bring us into the net; Thou didst lay an oppressive burden upon our loins. Thou didst make men ride over our heads; we went through fire and through water; yet Thou didst bring us out into a place of abundance. Come and hear, all who fear God, and I will tell you what He has done for my soul. I cried to Him with my mouth, and He was extolled with my tongue. If I regard wickedness in my heart, the Lord will not hear; but certainly God has heard; He has given heed to the voice of my prayer. Blessed be God, who has not turned away my prayer, nor His lovingkindness from me." Psalm 66:8-12, 16-20.* David suffered the loss of several close friends and three of his sons during trials in his life. His relationship with the Lord pulled him through. He praises God that his prayers were answered.

Prayer: Dear Lord of grace and tender mercies. Come to our rescue when we are weak and help us avoid the devils schemes which rage against us. Sometimes we get lost in our grief and are tempted to lose control and do things that may hurt us and dishonor you. Lord lead us to your escape route. Lord hear our prayers. Amen.

"But now I am going to Him who sent Me; and none of you ask Me, 'Where are You going?'" John 16:5.

"Before the throne of God above I have a strong and perfect plea,
A great High Priest whose name is love,
Who ever lives and pleads for me."
Lyrics from the song Before the Throne of God Above by Vikki Cook

Where is Jesus now and what is He doing there? Jesus told His disciples I am going to Him who sent Me. Jesus rose from the grave and ascended into Heaven where He now abides. The Bible tells us what He is doing there. *"Who is the one who condemns? Christ Jesus is He who died, yes, rather who was raised, who is at the right hand of God, who intercedes for us." Romans 8:34.* Jesus intercedes for us, speaking to the Father on our behalf.

The Apostle John writes, *"My little children, I am writing these things to you that you may not sin. And if anyone sins, we have an Advocate with the Father, Jesus Christ the righteous; and He Himself is the propitiation for our sins; and not ours only, but also for those of the whole world." 1 John 2:1-2.* Hallelujah! We have an Advocate with the Father who has sacrificed Himself to pay for our sins. Whenever we sin, Jesus stands before the Father shows His hands and side and says that one is not guilty. My blood has removed his sins.

The Apostle Paul writes to Timothy, *"This is good and acceptable in the sight of God our Savior, who desires all men to be saved and to come to the knowledge of the truth. For there is one God, and mediator also between God and men, the man Christ Jesus, who gave Himself as a ransom for all, the testimony borne at the proper time." 1 Timothy 2:3-6.* Praise God we have Jesus as our mediator who mediates a new covenant of grace and mercy. When we were sold into slavery to sin Jesus paid the ransom on the cross to set us free.

What about those who die in Christ, what happens to them? Where do they go when they leave this earth? Jesus responded to the thief who died on a cross next to Him who made this request, *"Jesus, remember me when You come in Your kingdom!" Jesus said to him, "Truly I say to you, today you shall be with Me in Paradise." Luke 23:42-43.* The thief on the cross had no hope, no way to redeem his sinful life from an eternity separated from God. He cries out a desperate prayer for mercy. Jesus' words, "you shall be with Me in Paradise", was his blessed answer. Hallelujah! What hope we have in Christ! We will be with Him in Paradise when our days are completed.

Paul writes these encouraging words: *"For we know that if the earthly tent which is our house is torn down, we have a building from God, a house not made with hands, eternal in the heavens. For indeed In this house we groan, longing to be clothed with our dwelling from heaven; Therefore, being always of good courage, and knowing that while we are at home in the body we are absent from the Lord – for we walk by faith, not by sight- we are of good courage, I say, and prefer to be absent from the body and to be at home with the Lord." 2 Corinthians 5:1-2, 6-8.* The older we get the more we tend to groan in our bodies, the more we long to be at home with the Lord.

Prayer: Lord Jesus, What a blessing it is to know that you there before our Father, interceding for us. Lord we thank you for the promise that to absent from the body is to be at home with You. Our loved ones who left us are now at home with You and when it is our time we will also dwell in Your presence. Lord, help us be faithful until we come home. Amen.

"But now I am going to Him who sent Me; and none of you ask Me, 'Where are You going?' But because I have said these things to you, sorrow has filled your heart." John 16:5-6.

Jesus breaks His disciples' hearts when He tells them that He is returning to the One who sent Him. In their hearts the Messiah was supposed to live forever. King David was given this Messianic promise by the Lord: *"When your days are complete and you lie down with your fathers, I will raise up your descendant after you, who will come forth from you, and I will establish his kingdom. He shall build a house for My name, and I will establish the throne of his kingdom forever." 2 Samuel 7:12-13.* According to these verses and the disciples' theology the Messiah was not supposed to go away. And here is Jesus, the Messiah, telling them that He was leaving. Over and over during His ministry Jesus told His disciples: *"The Son of Man is going to be delivered into the hands of men; and they will kill Him, and He will be raised on the third day." And they were deeply grieved. Matthew 17:22-23.* The cross was God's plan from the beginning, but it was deeply troubling to those who devoted themselves to Him. Even today, for those who love Jesus, the reading of the account of the crucifixion of their Lord brings tears to their eyes and conviction to their hearts. *"All of us like sheep have gone astray, each of us has turned to his own way; But the LORD has caused the iniquity of us all to fall on Him." Isaiah 53:6.* After the cross and resurrection of Jesus, the Apostle Peter preached these words on the Feast of Pentecost: *"This Man, delivered up by the predetermined plan and foreknowledge of God, you nailed to a cross by the hands of godless men and put Him to death. And God raised Him up again, putting an end to the agony of death, since it was impossible for Him to be held in its power. Therefore let all the house of Israel know for certain that God has made Him both Lord and Christ – this Jesus whom you crucified." Now when they heard this, they were pierced to the heart, and said to Peter and the rest of the apostles, "Brethren, what shall we do?" Acts 2:23-24, 36-37.* Three thousand Jews repented of their unbelief and were baptized as followers of Jesus on that day.

My daughter lost her first father to a sudden heart attack when she was just 7 years old. He was only 47 when this occurred. As a result she came to hate the word, "good-bye" and had great fear that she might lose her mother or I. When her mother went home to be with Jesus 12 years later her young heart could not bear the grief. I continue to pray for her that she might find comfort and peace in Jesus her Savior. My prayer for her is this; *"Now may the God of hope fill you with all joy and peace in believing, that you may abound in hope by the power of the Holy Spirit." Romans 15:13.*

Dear reader, *The Lord is near to the brokenhearted, and saves those who are crushed in spirit." Psalm 34:18.* May you know His closeness to you in your time of grief and be delivered from your crushed spirit.

Prayer: Dear Jesus, Thank You that You are both a heart breaker and a heart healer. Lord break us of the things that keep us from You and prevent the healing of our crushed spirits. Help us remember that You are *"A man of sorrows, and acquainted with grief; Surely our griefs You Yourself bore, and our sorrows You carried." Isaiah 53:3-4.* Jesus You did all this when You carried Your cross up a hill called Mount Calvary. Thank You for the knowledge that You promised, *"I will never desert you, nor will I ever forsake you." Hebrews 13:5.* Lord Jesus You are more than worthy of all of our praise and we look forward to the day when we worship You in person around Your throne in Heaven. Amen.

"But I tell you the truth, it is to your advantage that I go away; for if I do not go away, the Helper shall not come to you; but if I go, I will send Him to you." John 16:7.

"It is finished", Jesus said just before He died on the cross. Mission accomplished, the sacrifice has been made to atone for our sins. *"But He, (Jesus), having offered one sacrifice for sins for all time, sat down at the right hand of God. For by one offering He has perfected for all time those who are sanctified. And the Holy Spirit also bears witness to us; for after saying, 'This is the covenant that I will make with them after those days, says the LORD; I will put My laws upon their heart, and upon their mind I will write them'. He then says, 'And their sins and lawless deeds I will remember no more'. Now where there is forgiveness of these things, there is no longer any offering for sin.'" Hebrews 10:12, 14-18.* Hallelujah! The sacrifice has been made for our sins in Christ. And the Holy Spirit reminds us by putting God's law on our hearts and minds.

Not only that, the Holy Spirit prays for us when we are weak. *"And in the same way the Spirit also helps our weakness; for we do not know how to pray as we should, but the Spirit Himself intercedes for us with groanings too deep for words; and He who searches the hearts knows what the mind of the Spirit is, because He intercedes for the saints according to the will of God." Romans 8:26-27.* The Holy Spirit not only helps us by putting God's words on our hearts, He also prays for us when we cannot find the words.

John the Baptist pointed to Jesus and gave us this testimony: *"Behold, the Lamb of God who takes away the sin of the world! And I did not recognize Him, but He who sent me to baptize in water said to me, 'He upon whom you see the Spirit descending and remaining upon Him, this is the One who baptizes in the Holy Spirit.' And I have seen, and have borne witness that this is the Son of God."*

John 1:29, 33-34. Jesus has left this world, but He has baptized those who believe on Him with the Holy Spirit. The Spirit is He who comes along side us to help not only in time of need but every moment of every day.

Do you need help getting through your time of grief my friend? Call upon the Holy Spirit with faith in Jesus. You will find Him in your heart. *Now on the last day, the great day of the feast, Jesus stood and cried out, saying, "If any man is thirsty, let him come to Me and drink. He who believes in Me, as the Scripture said, 'From his innermost being shall flow rivers of living water.'" But this He spoke of the Holy Spirit, whom those who believed in Him were to receive. John 7:37-39.* When someone we love dies we tend to die with them, spiritually. We need to come to Jesus to receive the rivers of water flowing from our innermost being and start to live again. *But when the kindness of God our Savior and His love for mankind appeared, He saved us, not on the basis of deeds which we have done in righteousness, but according to His mercy, by the washing of regeneration and renewing by the Holy Spirit, whom He poured out upon us richly through Jesus Christ our Savior. Titus 3:4-6.* Do you need new life and renewal? The Holy Spirit is the One who ministers life-giving water to dry souls. Just surrender to His leading.

Prayer: Lord Jesus, thanks for the baptism of the Holy Spirit, who comes along side us to help us back up when we fall down in grief. Lord may our song always be: "I got a river of life flowing out of me." Lord Holy Spirit renew our hearts and regenerate our souls, for we are called to live to glorify Jesus, in whose name we pray, Amen.

"And He (the Holy Spirit), when He comes, will convict the world concerning sin, and righteousness, and judgment; concerning sin, because they do not believe in Me." John 16:8-9

"How blessed is he whose transgression is forgiven, whose sin is covered! How blessed is the man to whom the LORD does not impute iniquity, and in whose spirit is no deceit!." Psalm 32:1-2.

O what a blessed state to have peace with God! O the blessing of the conviction of the Holy Spirit of sin, which leads us to the throne of grace. Our sin causes the greatest grief and sorrow because it separates us from God. *"Behold, the LORD's hand is not so short that it cannot save; neither His ear so dull that it cannot hear. But your iniquities have made a separation between you and your God, and your sins have hidden His face from you, so that He does not hear." Isaiah 59:1-2.*

I love Billy Graham. He always told people that they were sinners separated from God. As a result the Holy Spirit convicted the hearts of many and they responded to the invitation to receive Jesus as their Savior. But conviction of sin does not come easy. Our resistance brings much pain and suffering. Listen to what King David went through after he had sinned. *"When I kept silent about my sin, my body wasted away through my groaning all day long. For day and night Thy hand was heavy upon me; my vitality was drained as with the fever heat of summer. I acknowledged my sin to Thee, and my iniquity I did not hide; I said, 'I will confess my transgressions to the LORD'; and Thou forgave the guilt of my sin." Psalm 32:3-5.*

As a believer we often sin and experience the separation of fellowship with God. We lack the blessing of the presence of the Lord in our lives. The Holy Spirit inside us is grieved and causes us grief until we come to repentance. *"Or do you think that the Scripture speaks to no purpose: 'He jealously desires the Spirit which He has made to dwell in us'? But He gives a greater grace. Therefore it says, 'God is opposed to the proud, but gives grace to the humble.' Submit therefore to God. Resist the devil and he will flee from you. Draw near to God and He will draw near to you. Cleanse your hands, you sinners; and purify your hearts, you double-minded. Be miserable and mourn and weep; let your laughter be turned into mourning, and your joy to gloom. Humble yourself in the presence of the Lord, and He will exalt you." James 4:5-10.* The Holy Spirit loves you and will not leave you alone until you repent and turn back to God.

"Martha therefore said to Jesus, 'Lord, if You had been here, my brother would not have died.'" John 11:21. Many of us who lose loved ones have passed on are so hurt by our loss that we fall into the sin of blaming God as if He had sinned against us. Some people take their grudges to the grave with them, living the rest of their lives in bitterness towards God. What a tragedy. It never has to be that way. Listen to what Job said after he lost all his children; *And he said, "Naked I came from my mother's womb, and naked I shall return there. The LORD gave and the LORD has taken away. Blessed be the name of the LORD." Through all this Job did not sin, nor did he blame God. Job 1:21-22.* I myself was angry and blamed God for taking away my wife Linda. But it just added to my sorrow until I submitted to God's will and found peace with Him. What a comfort I received from the Holy Spirit in my heart.

Prayer: Dear Holy Spirit, Thank You for Your conviction of sin. Thank You Jesus for the promise that our loved ones who know You are now safe in Your arms and like them we can have joy, peace, and sweet fellowship with You despite our grief. Blessed be the name of the Lord, Amen.

The Holy Spirit's Conviction of Righteousness, John 16:8, 10

*"And He (the Holy Spirit), when He comes, will convict the world concerning …
righteousness, … because I go to the Father, and you will no longer behold Me." John
16:8, 10*

What is righteousness? Righteousness is a word found throughout the entire Bible. God Himself is known to be perfectly righteous. Everything He says or does is right all of the time. People on the other hand are either considered righteous or unrighteous depending on their relationship with God based on their faith. Jesus taught, *"The good man out of the good treasure of his heart brings forth what is good; and the evil man out of the evil treasure brings forth what is evil; for the mouth speaks from that which fills the heart." Luke 6:45.*

Righteousness abides in the heart of the Lord Jesus. *"The LORD is righteous in all His ways, and kind in all His deeds. The LORD is near to all who call upon Him, to all who call upon Him in truth. He will fulfill the desire of those who fear Him; He will hear their cry and will save them." Psalm 145:17-19.* What a wonderfully righteous Savior is our Lord Jesus.

But what about us, how can we become righteous? God provided back in Old Testament days a way for His people, the Israelites, to acquire righteousness through obedience to His law given through Moses. *"So the LORD commanded us to observe all these statutes, to fear the LORD our God for our good always and for our survival, as it is today. And it will be righteousness for us if we are careful to observe all this commandment before the LORD our God, just as He commanded us." Deuteronomy 6:24-25.* But God's law proved impossible for the children of Israel or anyone else to obey.

Fortunately God provided a better way for us to become righteous. *"But now apart from the law the righteousness of God has been manifested, being witnessed by the law and the prophets, even the righteousness of God through faith in Jesus Christ for all those who believe; for there is no distinction; for all have sinned and fall short of the glory of God, being justified as a gift by His grace through the redemption which is in Christ Jesus; whom God displayed publically as a propitiation in His blood through faith. This was to demonstrate His righteousness, because in the forbearance of God He passed over the sins previously committed; for the demonstration, I say, of His righteousness at the present time, that He might be just and the justifier of the one who has faith in Jesus." Romans 3:21-26.* In simpler words righteousness is a gift of God provided through the sacrifice of Jesus for us on the cross. *"He (God) made Him (Jesus) who knew no sin to be sin on our behalf, that we might become the righteousness of God in Him." 2 Corinthians 5:21.* God made a deal on our behalf. He took our sin and placed them on Jesus and gave us His righteousness in exchange. Isn't He a wonderfully righteous God!

"For if by the transgression of the one, death reigned through the one, much more those who received the abundance of grace and the gift of righteousness will reign in life through the One, Jesus Christ. For as through the one man's disobedience the many were made sinners, even so through the obedience of the One the many will be made righteous." Romans 5:17, 19. And all we need to do is believe in the Lord Jesus Christ and we will be saved.

Prayer: Thank You Lord God that You provided a way through Your Son Jesus for us to receive Your precious gift of righteousness. O what wonderful news comes from the conviction of the Holy Spirit which leads to repentance and restores our relationship with God. Thank You precious Lord. Amen

But when He, the Spirit of truth, comes, He will guide you into all the truth; for He will not speak on His own initiative, but whatever He hears, He will speak; and He will disclose to you what is to come. John 16:13

When we go *through* a period of grieving after the loss of a loved one we tend to get disoriented and lost. Jesus looks down on us from heaven and sees us as distressed and downcast, like sheep without the guidance of a shepherd. We need someone to lead us, guide us and protect us.

When the LORD used Moses to lead the children of Israel out of slavery in Egypt He did not leave them to wander aimlessly. In Exodus 13:21-22 we read how the LORD's presence was with them. *"And the LORD was going before them in a pillar of cloud by day to lead them on the way, and a pillar of fire by night to give them light, that they might travel by day and by night. He did not take away the pillar of cloud by day, nor the pillar of fire by night, from before the people."* The LORD provided protection from Pharoah's army, as well as food and water so that they could survive in the barren wilderness. Through Moses God provided His Laws to guide them on how they should live for Him. Moses offers this testimony as to what happened in these song lyrics: *"In Thy lovingkindness Thou hast led the people whom Thou hast redeemed; In Thy strength Thou hast guided them to Thy holy habitation." Exodus 15:13.*

When Jesus came He led His disciples everywhere they went. He taught them how they should live for Him through His example and His teaching. Jesus spoke these words to assure them of His constant care for them: *"I am the good shepherd; and I know My own, and My own know Me, even as the Father knows Me and I know My Father; and I lay down My life for the sheep. My sheep hear My voice, and I know them, and they follow Me; and I give eternal life to them, and they shall never perish; and no one shall snatch them out of My hand." John 10:14-15, 27-28.* What a comfort it is to know this Good Shepherd who holds us securely in His hands.

But now since Jesus has gone to His Father in heaven, He leaves us the Holy Spirit to guide us into all truth. The first truth that the Spirit guides us is the truth that we are children of God. *"For all who are being led by the Spirit of God, these are sons of God. For you have not received a spirit of slavery leading to fear again. But you have received the spirit of adoption by which we cry out, 'Abba! Father!' The Spirit Himself bears witness with our spirit that we are children of God." Romans 8:14-16.*

God has not changed; as the LORD He went before the children of Israel in Exodus, then as Jesus He faithfully led His disciples as the good shepherd. Now God the Holy Spirit dwells in our hearts leading us in the ways of the Lord. We can now proclaim with the confidence of King David; *"Where can I go from Thy Spirit? Or where can I flee from Thy presence? If I ascend into heaven, Thou art there; if I make my bed in Sheol, behold, Thou art there. If I take the wings of the dawn, if I dwell in the remotest part of the sea, even there Thy hand will lead me and Thy right hand will lay hold of me." Psalm 139:7-10.* We can take the wise counsel of Solomon who wrote, *"Trust in the Lord with all your heart, and do not lean on your own understanding. In all your ways acknowledge Him, and He will make your paths straight." Proverbs 3:5-6.*

Prayer: Praise You Lord Jesus that we are not lost, but can follow You with confidence. We are grateful for the constant abiding presence of Your Holy Spirit who reminds that we are your children. Thank You for His guidance which helps us live godly lives and comforts us when we are distressed. Amen.

"A little while, and you will no longer behold Me; and again a little while, and you will see Me." John 16:16

When I read this verse I think of the many soldiers who say to their families when they leave for deployment to a far off country, "I'll be home soon". I recall the many videos of them returning home with joyful reunions with their wives and children. Those who know Jesus with loved ones who know Jesus who have gone to Heaven have the hope that they will in a little while have a joyful reunion with them.

"For if we believe that Jesus died and rose again, even so God will bring with Him those who have fallen asleep in Jesus. For the Lord Himself will descend from Heaven, with a shout, with the voice of the archangel, and with the trumpet of God; and the dead in Christ shall rise first. Then we who are alive and remain shall be caught up together with them in the clouds to meet the Lord in the air, and thus we shall always be with the Lord." 1 Thessalonians 4:14, 16-18

Jesus said, "again a little while, and you will see Me". Just like a soldier returning to his family our Lord is coming back with our lost loved ones with Him. Like a child waiting impatiently for their daddy to return, let's keep looking diligently for our Lord's return.

"Beyond the sunset, O glad reunion, With our dear loved ones who've gone before;
In that fair homeland, we'll know no parting, Beyond the sunset, forevermore!"
From hymn Beyond the Sunset
Text by Virgil P. and Blanche Brock

What a blessed old country hymn which reminds us of "the glad reunion" we have to look forward to. Hold on my grieving friends for in a little while we'll see Jesus and we will be home forever. Our brief separation shall be over for "we shall always be with the Lord."

Compared with the forever we will have in Heaven our time left on this earth will be brief.

"For I consider that the sufferings of this present time are not worthy to be compared with the glory that is to be revealed to us. And not only this, but also we ourselves, having the first fruits of the Spirit, even we ourselves groan within ourselves, waiting eagerly for our adoption as sons, the redemption of our body. For in hope we have been saved, but hope that is seen is not hope; for why does one hope for what he sees? But if we hope for what we do not see, with perseverance we wait eagerly for it." Romans 8:18, 23-25.

Friend let the hope we have in Christ help us endure the grief we are called to suffer. There will be glory revealed in us when we all get to Heaven. Our faith is not blind. It sees what we can't see with our eyes, the Jesus our loved ones we grieve for are now beholding.

Prayer: O Lord Jesus, We can't wait for your return. That blessed event can't happen soon enough. Lord, help us as the days of our separation may seem too long to us. Thanks for the comforting promise that "in a little while you will see Me".

Lord Jesus, be glorified in us. Amen.

"Truly, truly, I say to you, that you will weep and lament, but the world will rejoice; you will be sorrowful, but your sorrow will be turned to joy. Whenever a woman is in travail she has sorrow, because her hour has come; but when she gives birth to the child, she remembers the anguish no more, for joy that a child has been born into the world. Therefore you too now have sorrow; but I will see you again, and your heart will rejoice, and no one takes your joy away from you." John 16:20-22.

When you lose someone you dearly love unexpectedly at the age of 48, like I lost my wife, the grief and sorrow hits you very hard and can be overwhelming. The period of grief can last for years. But what I have experienced is that although the pain never goes away while we remain on this earth, the deep sorrow will eventually come to an end and the Lord will bring joy back to your heart. The Lord Himself is a joy restorer. He said, *"For I will turn their mourning into joy, and I will comfort them, and give them joy for their sorrow."* Jeremiah 31:13.

"Weeping may last for the night, but a shout of joy comes in the morning." Psalm 30:5.

"Those who sow in tears shall reap with joyful shouting." Psalm 126:5.

Hold on my sorrowful friend. Soon you will see Jesus. You will remember your anguish no more and your heart will rejoice will a joy that no one can take away.

Child bearing is a time of trial for most women. It ends usually with severe labor pains. But each mother receives relief when the job is done and a special joy when she finally holds her precious little one in her arms for the first time. Jesus promises His disciples a similar joy after they experience the grief of His departing. Each one of them endured great suffering during the rest of their lives as they brought the gospel of Jesus Christ to a dying world. But what a deeper joy they received when they were reunited with their Lord after their martyrdom. As Christians we have confidence that when we depart from this world we too will see our wonderful Savior. We who are left behind as mourners can rejoice with those who have departed knowing our loved one is enjoying the very presence of their Savior at this very moment. But we as mourners can turn to this same Savior and receive the comfort that only Jesus can give.

Prayer: Dear Jesus, Thanks for the promise You give that after our time of sorrow on this earth there will come an everlasting time of joy when we at last see your face. Thank You that You bring joy in the midst of our sorrows after we've said goodbye to our loved ones. Until then keep us close to Your side and guide us to our eternal home. For Your glory, Amen.

"Truly, truly I say to you. If you shall ask the Father for anything, He will give it to you in My name. Until now you have asked for nothing in My name; ask, and you shall receive, that your joy may be full." John 16:23-24.

The disciples of Jesus were about to face the trauma of the arrest, trial, and crucifixion of their beloved Lord. After His resurrection they will witness His departure into Heaven, leaving a major void in their lives. Jesus repeats the promise that, "If you shall ask the Father for anything, He will give it to you in My name, " four times in the upper room discourse .

Like the disciples, we Christians today are Jesus' faithful followers. His promises to us of our Father's love, answers to prayer, and His provisions are a source of great comfort to us. This is repeated several times throughout the New Testament. In Hebrews 4:16 we are encouraged to, *"Let us therefore draw near with confidence to the throne of grace, that we may receive mercy and find grace to help in time of need."*

Our greatest need is the presence of the Lord Himself. What a blessing to know that the door to His throne room is always open to us. Jesus says, *"Ask, and it shall be given to you; seek, and you shall find; knock, and it shall be opened to you. For everyone who asks receives, and he who seeks finds, and to him who knocks it shall be opened." Matthew 7:7-8.* If you ask, seek, and knock as Jesus exhorts us to, you will find our Heavenly Father to be faithful. Your testimony will be like Thomas O. Chisholm's when he wrote the hymn: Great is Thy Faithfulness. Great is Thy faithfulness! Great is Thy faithfulness! Morning by morning new mercies I see, all I have needed Thy hand hath provided – Great is Thy faithfulness, Lord unto me!"

My grieving friend, anxiety may fill your hearts and minds, but the Apostle Paul offers us the cure in Philippians 4:6-7. He writes, *"Be anxious for nothing, but in everything by prayer and supplication with thanksgiving let your requests be made known to God. And the peace of God, which surpasses all comprehension, shall guard your hearts and your minds in Christ Jesus."* Prayer to God gives us peace in times of anxiety and as Jesus promises, fullness of joy in the midst of great sorrow.

Our Lord calls out to us, *"Behold, I stand at the door and knock; if anyone hears My voice and opens the door, I will come in to him, and will dine with him, and he with Me. He who overcomes, I will grant to him to sit down with Me on My throne, as I also overcame and sat down with My Father on His throne." Revelation 3:20-21.*

Prayer is the door to the throne room of the Father and of Jesus. He knocks. Will you open and let Him in? What a blessing awaits us at the Throne of grace! A Father who loves us unconditionally, is always there for us, answers our prayers, and meets our every need. "Pardon from sin and a peace that endureth, Thy own dear presence to cheer and to guide; strength for today and bright hope for tomorrow, blessings all mine, with ten thousand beside!" Thomas O. Chisholm. May you often find yourself at the throne of grace my friend.

Prayer: Dear Lord Jesus, I open the door of my heart to You. Please come in and make Yourself at home. Thank You that You have died on the cross to take away my sins so that I now have access to Your Father. Please minister to my heart and mind the peace of God which surpasses all comprehension which You have promised to anxious souls who come to You in prayer. Amen.

"In that day you will ask in My name, and I do not say that I will request the Father on your behalf; for the Father Himself loves you, because you have loved Me, and have believed that I came forth from the Father. I came forth from the Father, and have come into the world; I am leaving the world again, and going to the Father." John 16:26-28.

The Father loves you. Take a few minutes to ponder these four words. What a blessing it is to know a perfect Father's love. The very one you pray to loves you. He knows your every need before you even ask. *"How precious is Thy lovingkindness, O God! And the children of men take refuge in the shadow of Thy wings." Psalm 36:7.* God is a Father who takes care of His children.

"Be gracious to me, O Lord. For to Thee I cry all day long. Make glad the soul of Thy servant, for to Thee, O Lord, I lift up my soul. For Thou, Lord, art good, and ready to forgive, and abundant in lovingkindness to all who call upon Thee. Give ear, O Lord, to my prayer; and give heed to my supplications! In the day of my trouble I shall call upon Thee, for Thou wilt answer me." Psalm 86:3-7

What confidence we have that our heavenly Father hears our prayers and ministers to our souls with unexpected answers.

"The LORD is compassionate and gracious, slow to anger and abounding in lovingkindness. For as high as the heavens are above the earth, so great is His lovingkindness toward those who fear Him. As far as the east is from the west, so far has He removed our transgressions from us. Just as a father has compassion on his children, so the LORD has compassion on those who fear Him." Psalm 103:8, 11-13.

Our Father is merciful to remove that which separates us from Him, our sins. He not only forgives them, He completely removes them. How did He do that? *"God demonstrates His own love toward us, in that while we were yet sinners, Christ died for us." Romans 5:8*

"By this the love of God was manifested in us, that God has sent His only begotten Son into the world so that we might live through Him. In this is love, not that we loved God, but the He loved us and sent His Son to be the propitiation for our sins." 1 John 4:9-10

God so loved us that He gave us His Son, Jesus, to die as a sacrifice for our sins. Our Father could not live without us. He sent Jesus to die in our place so that we can now know this God who loves us. God's love does not end when we are saved. It will continue throughout our entire lives and on into eternity.

"Give thanks to the LORD, for He is good; For His lovingkindness is everlasting. Psalm 118:1.

There is no end to our Father's love. It will never be exhausted. Nothing we can ever do will ever stop Him from loving us.*"This I recall to my mind, therefore I have hope.*

The LORD's lovingkindnesses indeed never cease, for His compassions never fail.
They are new every morning; great is Thy faithfulness.
'The LORD is my portion,' says my soul, Therefore I have hope in Him.'
The LORD is good to those who wait for Him, To the person who seeks Him." Lamentations 3:21-25

Prayer: Our Father, We praise You for Your love for us which has no end. Lord we thank You for Your goodness and lovingkindness in redeeming us by the blood of Your Son. How awesome You are O Lord. Thank You that You are attentive to our prayers and always answer according to what is best for us. Amen.

Jesus answered them, "Do you now believe? Behold, an hour is coming, and now has already come, for you to be scattered, each to his own home, and to leave Me alone; and yet I am not alone, because the Father is with Me," John 16:31-32

"O you of little faith, why did you doubt?" Jesus said this to Peter as He pulled him out of the Sea of Galilee. In fact Jesus pointed out the littleness of His disciples' faith seven times in the Gospels. At the end of His Upper Room Discourse with His disciples, Jesus again questions their faith in Him. *"Do you now believe?"* Jesus knew the hearts of His disciples. He also knew how they would respond to His arrest. He knew that they would abandon Him when He needed prayer partners. Jesus prayed alone in the Garden of Gethsemane. Jesus said to them, *"So, you men could not keep watch with Me for one hour?" Matthew 26:40.*

Jesus had said to His disciples earlier, *"You will all fall away because of Me this night, for it is written, 'I will strike down the shepherd, and the sheep of the flock shall be scattered.'" Matthew 26:31.* When the Judas led mob arrived to arrest Jesus, He said, *"Have you come out with swords and clubs to arrest Me as against a robber? Every day I used to sit in the Temple teaching and you did not seize Me. But all this has taken place that the Scripture of the prophets may be fulfilled." Then all the disciples left Him and fled". Matthew 26:55-56.*

Jesus did not resist arrest. He knew it was His Father's will. When the disciples saw this, they skedaddled away as quickly as they could. Who could blame them, without Jesus they were powerless against an armed and angry mob. Fear and wisdom prevailed as they abandoned the Messiah whom they had put their faith in.

When we lose a loved one we also have a tendency to temporarily lose our faith. And we tend to forget the Lord who loves us and redeemed us from the pit of despair. We forget about the Holy Spirit who Jesus baptized us with when we first put our faith in Him. Jesus promised this same Holy Spirit to His disciples after His resurrection. Just before He ascended back to Heaven Jesus spoke to them. *After gathering them together, He commanded them not to leave Jerusalem, but to wait for what the Father had promised, "Which," He said, "you heard of from Me; for John baptized with water, but you shall be baptized with the Holy Spirit not many days from now. But you shall receive power when the Holy Spirit has come upon you; and you shall be My witnesses both in Jerusalem, and in all Judea and Samaria, and even to the remotest part of the earth." Acts 1:4-5, 8.*

The despair of the disciples was short lived. When they received the outpouring of the Holy Spirit that was promised to the disciples, they went from down and out to joyfully and boldly making Jesus known to people who spoke languages they did not know. The disciples preached the Good News of the resurrection of Jesus and saw thousands of people come to faith in their Messiah, Jesus.

Regardless of our current circumstances, we all have the same calling and His Holy Spirit dwelling in us to accomplish it. Your loved one has been called home and you have been left behind to fulfill a mission. You can have your grieving heart renewed by an outpouring of the Holy Spirit and perhaps find a new and more glorious purpose for your life, serving our Lord Jesus.

Prayer: Dear Jesus, Thank You that despite the disciples' lack of faith, that You never stopped loving them and You restored their faith and joy after great sorrow. Thank You, Jesus, for the renewing power of Your Holy Spirit who is always with us, restoring us, and empowering us to overcome our grief and giving us new life in You. May we shine until it is our turn to go home! To Your Glory, Amen.

We Have Peace Because Jesus has Overcome the World John 16:33

"These things I have spoken to you, that in Me you may have peace. In the world you have tribulation, but take courage; I have overcome the world." John 16:33.

Jesus sure was right about us, His disciples, having tribulation in this world. Everywhere we look there is much suffering and death. Every day in the news we hear about somebody who killed somebody else. Wars and mass murder add to the great body count. The value of human life is diminishing. Disease is getting more rampant. Several of my closest friends have recently gone home to be with the Lord. My wife, Linda, suffered during the whole eleven years of our married life. It seems that every week she was in the hospital.

In addition to all the suffering going on in this world, sin is abounding more and more as moral standards drift away from God's word. Jesus said, *"For the coming of the Son of Man will be just like the days of Noah." Matthew 24:37.* What were people like in the days of Noah? Genesis 6: 5-6, 11 answers our question; *"Then the LORD saw that the wickedness of man was great on the earth, and that every intent of the thoughts of his heart was only evil continually. And the LORD was sorry that He had made man on the earth, and He was grieved in His heart. Now the earth was corrupt in the sight of God, and the earth was filled with violence."* Now doesn't that sound just like our world today. The Apostle Paul gives us this pathetic prophetic outlook, *"But realize this, that in the last days difficult times will come. For men will be lovers of self, lovers of money, boastful, arrogant, revilers, disobedient to parents, ungrateful, unholy, unloving, irreconcilable, malicious gossips, without self-control, brutal, haters of good, treacherous, reckless, conceited, lovers of pleasure rather than lovers of God." 2 Timothy 3:1-4.* There is much suffering and death in this world due to the evil in the hearts of the creatures who are made in the image of God. It seems that every month mass murders are committed somewhere in this world. Is there any hope? Is there an answer to the ills of this world?

Yes. There is hope. His name is Jesus who said, *"Take courage; I have overcome the world."* Jesus overcame sin by being the sacrifice which takes away our sin when He died on His cross. What did Jesus accomplish on the cross? The Apostle Paul tells us what Christ's death did for our sins. *"And when you were dead in your transgressions and the uncircumcision of your flesh, He made you alive together with Him, having forgiven us all our transgressions, having cancelled out the certificate of debt consisting of decrees against us; and He has taken it out of the way, having nailed it to the cross. When He had disarmed the rulers and authorities, He made a public display of them, having triumphed over them through Him." Colossians 2:13-15.* Hallelujah! Our sins died with Christ when He died on the cross. They no longer have power over us. We have been set free.

It gets even better. Jesus' life did not end at the cross. On the third day He rose up from the tomb a victor over death. Praise the Lord! Because He has overcome sin and death, we too can overcome sin and death and live with Jesus forever. Jesus will also bring an end to all the suffering and sin in this world when He returns.

Prayer: Thank You Jesus, For the victory You have achieved at the cross and the empty tomb. Not only are You sinless and imperishable, You have set us free from sin and death. We look forward to an awesome future with You, Jesus, and with everyone who called You Lord. Forever, with grateful hearts we will sing Your praise. Jesus, Your name be praised forever! Amen.

Be still, my soul! The Lord is on thy side; Bear patiently the cross of grief or pain;
Leave to thy God to order and provide; In every change He faithful will remain.
Be still, my soul! Thy best, thy heavenly Friend Thro' thorny ways leads to a joyful end.
Be still, my soul! Thy God doth undertake to guide the future as He has the past.
Thy hope, thy confidence let nothing shake; all now mysterious shall be bright at last.
Be still, my soul! The waves and winds still know
His voice who ruled them while He dwelt below.
Be still, my soul! The hour is hastening on when we shall be forever with the Lord,
When disappointment, grief, and fear are gone, sorrow forgot, love's purest joys restored.
Be still, my soul! When change and tears are past, all safe and blessed we shall meet at last.
Be Still, My Soul, by Katharina von Schlegel

Printed in the United States
By Bookmasters